HIGHER

Business Management

Case Studies and Exam Preparation

Peter Hagan
Rhona Sivewright
Alistair B. Wylie

Hodder Gibson
A MEMBER OF THE HODDER HEADLINE GROUP

The Publishers would like to thank the following for permission to reproduce copyright material:
Photo credits
Page 4 © Burns Express; page 5 © Firefly Productions/Corbis; page 10 © FLPA/Holt Studios/Bob Gibbons; pages 14 and 15 © Hodder Education; pages 20 and 21 © BAA plc; page 25 © Photofusion Picture Library/Alamy; page 26 © Scottish Cashmere Club; page 30 © Andy Arthur/Alamy; pages 35 and 36 © Baxters Food Group; pages40 and 41 © D.C.Thomson & Co Ltd; page 45 © Tilly Confectionery; page 46 © Scottish Food & Drink/Scottish Enterprise; page 50 © www.purestockX.com; page 51 © FAN travelstock/Alamy; page 55 © Mark Sykes/Alamy; page 56 © Cephas Picture Library/Alamy; page 60 © Lingo24 Translation Services/www.lingo24.com; page 61 © The Royal Bank of Scotland; page 65 © BAA; page 66 © Paul Rapson/Alamy; page 70 © Andrew Linscott/Alamy; page 72 © Gary Roebuck/Alamy; pages 75 and 76 © Hodder Education.

Acknowledgements
Every effort has been made to trace all copyright holders, but if any have been inadvertently overlooked the Publishers will be pleased to make the necessary arrangements at the first opportunity.

Orders: please contact Bookpoint Ltd, 130 Milton Park, Abingdon, Oxon OX14 4SB. Telephone: (44) 01235 827720. Fax: (44) 01235 400454. Lines are open 9.00 – 5.00, Monday to Saturday, with a 24-hour message answering service. Visit our website at www.hoddereducation.co.uk. Hodder Gibson can be contacted direct on: Tel: 0141 848 1609; Fax: 0141 889 6315; email: hoddergibson@hodder.co.uk

First published in 2006 by
Hodder Gibson, an imprint of Hodder Education,
a member of the Hodder Headline Group
2a Christie Street
Paisley PA1 1NB

Impression number 5 4 3 2
Year 2010 2009 2008 2007

Cover photo (and running graphic) © Photodisc
Illustrations by DC Graphic Design Limited
Typeset in 10.5pt New Century Schoolbook by DC Graphic Design Limited, Swanley Village, Kent.
Printed and bound in Great Britian by Martins The Printers, Berwick-upon-Tweed

A catalogue record for this title is available from the British Library

ISBN-13: 978-0-340-91474-8

CONTENTS

Introduction

Welcome to *Higher Business Management Case Studies and Exam Preparation.*

This book is intended as a companion to *Higher and Intermediate 2 Business Management.* It has been written in simple and everyday language wherever possible, and is intended for use by students and teachers alike.

The authors are experienced educators with over 50 years' of teaching experience between them in the secondary, further and higher education sectors, as well as the national education arena. The authors have also marked and examined Business Management at Higher level since its inception.

This book comprises 15 case studies set to the standard of Section One of the Higher level external assessment, 45 examples of questions set to the standard of Section Two of the Higher level external assessment, suggested outline answers to case studies and questions, and useful tips for exam preparation and coverage of the construction of the external paper.

The book is divided into four sections:

- **Tips on examination preparation and the construction of the exam paper**
- **Section One Case studies and questions**
- **Section Two Questions**
- **Suggested solutions to all case studies and questions**

It should be noted that suggested solutions to all case studies and questions are provided in an abbreviated format and are not exhaustive in nature. Other answers may be acceptable in addition to those suggested. The answers provided give a summary of some of the main points that the authors believe should be contained in a good answer, and are given in a bulleted format for ease of reference. The command word used in each question should also be reflected and given due consideration in the answer. Note that this is not covered in the abbreviated format solutions.

We are indebted to our families for their patience during the writing of this book and to our friends, colleagues and peers for their advice and encouragement in its preparation. Special thanks must also go to the staff at Hodder Gibson, Paisley. In particular, John Mitchell for his unwavering support for the book, and Katherine Bennett for her due diligence and patience in dealing with us and proofing the book before publication.

We, the authors, hope that you will find this a useful resource during your period of study and preparation for external examination in the subject.

Peter Hagan

Rhona Sivewright

Alistair B Wylie

May 2006

Preparing for the external assessment

Part of your preparation for the external assessment should include familiarity with the construction of the examination paper.

The external assessment for Higher Business Management is one paper with a duration of two hours and 30 minutes. The paper is split into two sections: Section One and Section Two. The paper is marked out of 100 marks.

Section One of the paper is worth 50 marks and is based on a case study. This section is **compulsory** and you must attempt to answer all of the questions. The case study will be based on a real life organisation or industry and will usually be Scottish-based. The information presented will be about 750 words in length. You must make sure that you read this carefully **before** attempting any questions. Section One Question 1 is **always** phrased in exactly the same way and is **always** worth 10 marks:

> 'Identify the **problems** faced by … … … … … Use the following headings.
> (Please identify problems only; solutions will not be credited.)'

It should normally be possible to identify about six problems (which would be awarded six marks) with relative ease from the case study. The remaining problems/marks will be harder to identify and this is part of the differentiation built into the question paper. This means that some marks will be relatively straightforward for all candidates to find, but the remaining marks which differentiate between 'B' and 'A' Grade candidates will be more difficult to gain.

Section One Question 1 (10 marks) always relates directly to the case study, although the remaining 40 marks that make up Section One do not have to relate directly to the case study, and nor do your answers. There will usually be a total of between five and eight questions to answer in Section One of the question paper in addition to Question 1. The questions can cover topics from any part of the Course.

Section Two of the question paper introduces some degree of choice. There are five questions, each worth 25 marks, from which you must choose and answer two questions. Topics are integrated throughout the questions, with most questions covering an average of three topic areas. It is therefore not possible to study only part of the Course and hope to pass the external assessment. Topic areas which are covered in the compulsory Section One are unlikely to be covered again in Section Two.

You should read all 5 questions carefully before deciding on the 2 questions which you are going to attempt. It is important to read every question carefully, as you may begin to answer a question only to discover that you are unable to answer a substantial number of marks on a topic which is your weak area. Choose questions which present topics that you are able to answer and score highly with confidence to maximise your overall score for the assessment.

When writing your answers to any question in this examination, it is essential that you **answer the question that is asked**. This may sound fairly obvious, but many candidates fail because they write down what they know about a topic, rather than answering what the question has asked them about the topic.

When answering questions, it is also advisable to write your answer in sentences and paragraphs. Bulleted lists of words are not normally acceptable at Higher level without further explanation. You may, however, wish to present your answer using bullet points, with sentences or paragraphs presented in a list format.

The SQA has issued a list of command words which are used in Higher Business Management to assist both teachers and candidates. Typically, every question contains a command word, around which your answer should be constructed. The list gives the meanings for the command words which are used in the external assessment. It is essential that you make yourself familiar with these words, their meanings and how to answer questions in the examination. Your classroom teacher should be able to help you with this part of examination technique. The list of command words follows.

Command word	Definition
Compare	Identify similarities and differences between two or more factors.
Describe	Provide a thorough description.
Discuss	Examine closely taking account of strengths and weaknesses in an argument; for and against.
Distinguish	Identify the differences between two or more factors.
Explain	A detailed response (definition and explanation) as to how/why something may benefit/hinder.
Identify	Give the name or identifying characteristics of something.
Justify	Give reasons to support suggestions, conclusions.
Outline	State the main features.

SECTION ONE

Case Studies

Case Study 1 Burns Express

Case Study 2 Soft Fruit

Case Study 3 Robert Wiseman Dairies

Case Study 4 Aberdeen Airport

Case Study 5 Cashmere

Case Study 6 Shipbuilding

Case Study 7 Baxters Foods

Case Study 8 DC Thomson

Case Study 9 Tilly Confectionary

Case Study 10 Thomson Holidays

Case Study 11 Scottish Whisky

Case Study 12 Lingo24

Case Study 13 BAA

Case Study 14 Dairy Farmers

Case Study 15 McCowans Highland Toffee

CASE STUDY 1

Burns Express

This section should take you approximately one hour and 15 minutes.

Read through the following information, then answer the questions which follow.

Burns Express Freight Ltd is a leading provider of logistical solutions based near Glasgow Airport. It has expanded rapidly since formation in 1993.

The main focus of the company has always been customer service. This has led to a diversification of services provided by the company over recent years, in order to satisfy an ever-changing market. The 'same day' market, which used to be the mainstay of the company when it was initially formed, is no longer as buoyant as it once was.

USING ICT IN BUSINESS

Advances in information technology mean that there is now less urgency to transport freight from A to B. Companies are always looking at the most cost-effective methods of moving freight, and are not willing to spend money on an expensive dedicated delivery service. This is particularly true when the economy is slow and money is tight.

An example of cost-effective transport is the growth in 'pallet networks'. Using this kind of method, freight is shipped overnight to a central hub from all areas of the UK, and grouped together into various distribution areas. It is then collected by the pallet network members for each area for delivery the following day. Pooling resources in this way can be an effective method of cutting costs and increasing turnover.

There are occasions however when a shipment is of too high a value or too fragile to go through the rigours of this system. On these occasions, companies have no choice but to send this freight in a dedicated vehicle at greater cost.

In order to satisfy both customer and market demand, and also to remain competitive, new technology has been embraced in the form of satellite tracking of vehicles and computerised traffic management systems.

Costs can be monitored using both these systems, ensuring that the company can provide a cost-effective service to its customers and still maintain a realistic level of profitability. There are added benefits to the customer: e.g. freight can be tracked from A to B, removing concerns over loss; this again helps the company to retain a competitive edge.

RECRUITING NEW STAFF

Due to the growth in turnover and also as a result of the diversification of services within the company (provision of new services like Parcel deliveries and an Irish Groupage Service), there has also been a requirement to recruit additional drivers and administrative staff. Vacancies were advertised in both the local newspaper and jobcentre. The structure of the company was changed and new departments formed, to split the workload and create dedicated staff as a main point of contact for each area. This ensures that any customer enquiry or query can be directed to the correct department and dealt with more quickly and efficiently.

PURCHASING NEW VEHICLES

Even the purchase of certain vehicles within the company is usually a customer-led decision, in that certain criteria have to be met for certain customers. This can range from the size of vehicle to how much the vehicle can transport, in terms of volume and weight. In certain cases there is a limit to the age of vehicle that can be used. In order to keep within these limits, the company has an age policy on vehicles and renews its fleet every three years. As all vehicles are liveried with the company logo and contact details, they present a good image to customers and also act as the company's 'advertising on wheels'. Other forms of advertising utilised by the company are direct marketing using printed brochures, and regular mailshots to targeted companies. The company website also provides basic details of services provided and contact information. In addition to this a Business Development Manager has recently been recruited, taking overall responsibility for general marketing and generating new business.

Case Study continues over the page

NEW INVESTMENT

All of the initial costs for additional investment were originally financed by retained profits within the company. As the level of investment has increased and been planned as an ongoing process, it has become necessary to approach the company bankers for additional funding in the form of an invoice discounting facility. This effectively means that the bank 'buys' the company's debtors and pays 80 per cent of any customer debt immediately on it being invoiced. This is an increasingly common form of finance for companies, which greatly improves cashflow as there is no delay in waiting for customers to pay. Credit terms are normally 30 days, although it is not uncommon for modern business practice to allow up to 60 days for payment to be received.

The investment in technology, equipment and human resources over recent years is planned to be an ongoing project. The company is continually looking at new developments such as handheld scanners and enhanced traffic software to ascertain if they will be an added benefit, either immediately or in the future. As the company grows it will continue to invest in all these areas as a necessary requirement, rather than class it as a luxury. This will ensure that standards are maintained and allow the company to continue to be a market leader in its field.

QUESTIONS

You should note that although the following questions are based on the stimulus material, it does not contain all the information needed to provide suitable answers to all the questions. You will need to make use of knowledge you have acquired while studying the course.

Answer ALL the questions.

Marks

1 Identify the problems faced by Burns Express Freight Ltd. **10**
Use the following headings. (Please identify problems only, solutions will not be credited.)

- human resources
- operations
- marketing
- external

2 Burns Express Freight Ltd funded part of its expansion using retained profits.

(a) Describe the costs and benefits of using internal finance compared to external finance. **4**

(b) Describe two other types of support that may be available to businesses. **2**

3 Burns Express Freight Ltd employs a variety of ICT equipment in the running of the business.

(a) Outline the costs and benefits of using ICT in business. **4**

(b) Explain why the use of ICT may influence decision-making in the business. **5**

4 Burns Express Freight Ltd use direct marketing techniques to raise customer awareness.

Describe three other methods used by businesses to market their products and services. **3**

5 Burns Express Freight Ltd is concerned with maintaining quality of service and being a market leader.

(a) Describe the benefits to a business and its customers of exercising strict quality management. **5**

Marks

(*b*) State the four main methods of transport of goods used in the UK today, and describe the costs and benefits of two of them. **6**

6 Burns Express Freight Ltd operates a hierarchical structure.

Describe two other forms of organisational structure. **4**

7 Burns Express Freight Ltd uses a lot of ICT in the operation of its business.

Identify and describe two different types of training that may be used to update staff on the use of new equipment. **3**

8 Describe four external influences which may affect the operation of a business. **4**

(50)

Soft Fruit

This section should take you approximately one hour and 15 minutes.

Read through the following information, then answer the questions which follow.

LATE RASPBERRY CROP LEAVES STORES WAITING

Marks and Spencer feel that they could be selling more raspberries but are eagerly awaiting the ripening of the Scottish crop. This is welcome news to the fruit growers, as only a year ago they struggled to sell their crop. This was due to competition from English growers and a general fall in consumer demand. Successful promotions have increased this demand, but unfortunately this year's Scottish crop is late. Lack of supplies may force the price of the product upwards.

Soft fruit has become enormously important to all the multiple retailers within the UK. The market has grown by a phenomenal 48 per cent with blueberries proving to be the fastest growing sector.

Even during the winter months, strawberries, raspberries and blueberries sell well. Out of season, the fruit is sourced from warmer countries. However, British products are popular with consumers who rate the fruit as having a superior taste. Labelling as to the country of origin is vital, as consumers will not be aware of the different variety of fruit plants used.

RESEARCH AND DEVELOPMENT

Large amounts of money is spent on researching ways to protect crops from pests and diseases. Attempts at developing new varieties of plants are also being made.

Research is also being carried out with regard to the fruit picking. In a labour-intensive industry, speed of picking is important, as is the need to pick the fruit without damaging it. Some work has taken place with regard to mechanised picking but this proved difficult when picking fruit suitable for the supermarket, where it is marketed as a high value fresh product. Mechanised picking may be satisfactory for fruit required for the production of jam and jellies. However, this is no longer an important outlet for the UK growers. Canning strawberries in the UK lost popularity 25 years ago when the industry faced heavy competition from Poland. In addition to this, jam and jelly are not as popular with UK consumers as they once were. Canned fruit is now less popular than it used to be due to the wide availability of the fresh product.

Case Study continues over the page

PICKING THE FRUIT

A CD-based information pack has been produced for pickers. Issued in seven different languages, it reflects the nationalities of fruit pickers. This labour force often consists of students, many of whom come from Eastern European countries. Many years ago, school children would pick fruit in their school holidays. They were paid for each kilogram of fruit which they picked. The piece rate method of payment meant that the harder the pickers worked, the more money they earned. Seasonal work suited the children but proved less popular with adults looking for long-term employment. The job itself proved too monotonous for many people after several days of picking fruit.

Growing fruit under cover, using polytunnels, is also successful. It reduces the amount of fruit spoiled by rain and eaten by birds.

DISTRIBUTION

Angus Fruits started in 1994 as a family consortium. The family business has now grown to include 20 growers in Scotland and others in Spain, Portugal and Morroco. Ninety-five per cent of the crop is grown under polythene. In 2005 the company expects a turnover of £25 million, and to supply 10–15 per cent of the UK market. In the packing department, they employ no fewer than 2,000 students. They pick 4,000 tonnes of strawberries and 1,000 tonnes of raspberries in the UK. Later in the season, they will handle 4,000 tonnes of strawberries from Spain and North Africa.

It is now necessary to supply retailers with soft fruit for 12 months in the year. Due to the nature of the product, it is essential to keep the supply chain as short as possible to transport the product from the grower to the retailer while still fresh. Quality products are essential in this market. The Arbroath-based firm distributes fruit to 30 different supermarkets every night.

Developing new products is important. A variety has been developed which stays on the husk longer, which is important for the look of the product. It is also desirable for plants to produce fruit for a long time during the season, with successive plantings cropping from May to October.

Fruit farming has proved to be a real growth area in Scottish agriculture in recent years.

'PICK YOUR OWN'

Many fruit farms display signs at the roadside encouraging consumers to visit the farms. They may purchase fruit already picked for them or choose to pick their own fruit fresh from the fields. This has proved to be a successful family day out. Some farms have chosen to open cafes and shops, allowing customers to purchase products such as jam produced from the fruit.

Adapted from *The Courier and Advertiser*, 15 July 2005

QUESTIONS

You should note that although the following questions are based on the stimulus material, it does not contain all the information needed to provide suitable answers to all the questions. You will need to make use of knowledge you have acquired while studying the course.

Answer ALL the questions.

Marks

1 Identify the problems faced by the soft-fruit growers. Use the following headings. (Please identify problems only, solutions will not be credited.) **10**

- marketing
- operations
- human resources

2 Scottish fruit growers attempt to market their product as a superior, high quality product.

(a) Explain three marketing techniques which can be used to promote products as high quality. **3**

(b) Describe an effective system of quality assurance for a food producer. **6**

3 Describe the factors affecting the choice of delivery method for organisations. **4**

4 Explain the importance of research and development to producers. **4**

5 Many farms have extended their product life cycle and now offer consumers the chance to purchase jams and other products when they visit the farms.

Describe two alternative methods of extending a product life cycle. **4**

6 Piece rate is one method of paying staff for their work. Compare this with hourly rate as a means of achieving high quality output. **4**

7 Finance was required to invest in mechanisation.

(a) Describe two sources of finance which would enable large capital investment to take place. **4**

(b) Explain how managers might recognise if their investment had been worthwhile. **2**

		Marks
8	Describe two forms of legislation which affect the production of food products.	**4**
9	A CD-based information pack was produced for the fruit pickers. Discuss the use of ICT in training staff.	**5**
		(50)

Robert Wiseman Dairies

This section should take you approximately one hour and 15 minutes.

Read through the following information, then answer the questions which follow.

Robert Wiseman Dairies, has grown with bewildering speed. It now turns over more than £400 million, employs 3,000 staff and controls 20 per cent of the UK milk market.

The company's most recent results were equally impressive: interim profits grew by 21 per cent to £13.5 million.

It is no surprise that Robert Wiseman has been named UK entrepreneur of the year by accountants Ernst and Young.

BROTHERS IN ARMS

Mr Wiseman has an impressive legacy to live up to.

The Robert Wiseman of the company's name, the present boss's father, sold his farmland in 1947 to become the designated milk distributor for the new town of East Kilbride, on the southern fringe of Glasgow.

The Wiseman delivery schedule grew along with East Kilbride, graduating in the process from a horse and cart to electric milk floats.

It was when brothers Alan and Robert came on board in the 1970s that the firm took off. They took the view – revolutionary at the time – that doorstep deliveries were in decline, and that the future was in supplying retailers.

SPENDING UP

This shift called for heavy investment in new production, packaging and distribution facilities, at a time when bigger rivals such as Dairy Crest and Express Dairies were allowing their plants to age gracefully.

Wiseman also poured effort into branding, creating a highly distinctive black-and-white cowhide livery that runs from its cartons to its delivery trucks.

Because supermarkets kept driving down prices, the firm was forced to seek growth through acquisitions.

Since the beginning of the 1980s, Wiseman has taken over 54 companies.

THE BILLION-BOTTLE BOYS

Little wonder, then, that growth rates have been spectacular.

At the beginning of the 1990s, the company sold less than 100 million litres of milk; this year, it surpassed 1 billion litres for the first time.

In 1994, Wiseman had two per cent of the UK market; now, it has 20 per cent, with more than half its turnover coming from south of the border.

The firm's shares, listed in London in 1994, have more than doubled over the past three years, far outpacing its rivals.

Wiseman built a modern plant in Manchester, and then one in Droitwich, West Midlands, in 2001.

A map on the wall of Mr Wiseman's office charts the southward march, showing the business heading towards the big area it has yet to penetrate – the teeming millions of London and the southeast.

LIQUID ASSETS

Wiseman's success, analysts say, is the result of the firm's extraordinarily single-minded focus on its core business.

The firm has ruthlessly stripped away any distracting sidelines – tempting sources of added value such as cheese or yoghurt – from its business, leaving it only interested in selling liquid milk.

Wiseman's headquarters are still in the modest suburban farmhouse where Mr Wiseman senior set up shop.

'It's important to stick to what you know and not get sidelined,' says Douglas Nisbet, managing partner in Scotland for Ernst & Young. 'Since their shares have been listed, it's become especially important to be able to capture precisely what the firm is about in a couple of sentences.'

Case Study continues over the page

POLITICAL PROBLEMS

But the once-placid dairy sector is becoming ever more problematic.

Firstly, 'the milk business is hugely political', says Professor Donald McQueen, a specialist in the dairy industry at Glasgow University.

Imminent reforms to the EU's common agricultural policy are likely to cause a dramatic fall in UK milk production, shaking up Mr Wiseman's so-far amicable relations with suppliers. Pressure on prices is pulling in several directions: farmers in particular are becoming more strident in their demands for a bigger slice of the profits.

Regulators are nosing around eagerly: Wiseman faces a probe by the Competition Commission into alleged price-fixing in a slice of its Scottish business.

TIGHTENING UP

Secondly, opportunities for growth are not as obvious as they were.

The market, says Nicola Mallard, analyst at Investec Securities, 'is settling down into comfortable old age'.

Milk demand is at best stagnant, and no one expects it to pick up in the conceivable future.

In October, Danish-based Arla won permission to take over Express Dairies, creating a group which controls just over one-third of the British milk market.

With Dairy Crest controlling another 24 per cent and Wiseman on 20 per cent, that does not leave a great deal of room for further acquisitions.

At Ernst & Young, Mr Nisbet warns that Mr Wiseman may face a challenge in keeping the business focused as it grows.

'You have to keep the culture and ethos of the organisation intact', he says.

BREATHING SPACE

But Mr Wiseman could still be feasting on the cream for a while yet.

The Arla merger is likely to see various bits and pieces come onto the market: the firms have pledged to cut their capacity by one-quarter, which will provide a steady stream of morsels for Wiseman to snap up.

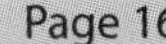

Overall, the UK market has around 20 per cent overcapacity in dairy processing: the fact that Wiseman, unlike its rivals, has modern, efficient plants means that it is unlikely to be pushed into cutting back production.

Overall, says Mr Wiseman, 'there is no reason why we shouldn't have 30 per cent of the market in the near future'.

***BBC News*, 2 December 2003**

Questions

You should note that although the following questions are based on the stimulus material, it does not contain all the information needed to provide suitable answers to all the questions. You will need to make use of knowledge you have acquired while studying the course.

Answer ALL the questions.

		Marks
1	Identify the problems faced by Wiseman dairies both past and present. Use the following headings. (Please identify problems only, solutions will not be credited.) • marketing • operations • finance • other	**10**
2	Wiseman has acquired 54 other companies since the beginning of the 1980s.	
	(a) Identify and describe two methods of growth.	**6**
	(b) Outline external factors that could restrict the growth of an organisation.	**4**
3	Wiseman became a public limited company in 1994.	
	(a) Discuss the advantages and disadvantages for an organisation of becoming a public limited company.	**5**
	(b) Other than selling shares, describe two other methods of long-term finance to fund the growth of a business.	**4**
4	Milk has to be processed and delivered quickly to ensure that it is still fresh when it reaches the supermarket shelves. Explain the factors to be considered when deciding on a system of distribution and delivery for an organisation.	**5**
5	Wiseman has contracts with some of the major supermarkets.	
	(a) Discuss the advantages and disadvantages of using a customer grouping when dealing with a few big clients.	**4**
	(b) Compare two other types of grouping.	**4**

Marks

6 Wiseman has a large number of employees and a large wage bill.

(a) Compare two different payment systems which an organisation may use for employees. **4**

(b) Describe methods other than pay that an organisation can use to motivate employees. **4**

(50)

C A S E   S T U D Y   4

Aberdeen Airport

This section should take you approximately one hour and 15 minutes.

Read through the following information, then answer the questions which follow.

ABERDEEN AIRPORT

Aberdeen Airport is one of seven UK airports owned by the British Airports Authority (BAA plc). The airport was opened in 1935 and is located seven miles from the city. When the airport opened it was surrounded by countryside, but the development of the city means that housing is now located near to the airport. It has one main passenger terminal, and two which are specifically used for the numerous helicopters serving the North Sea oil rigs. Aberdeen is the largest oil-related centre in Europe. Last year, 2.5 million passengers used Aberdeen airport.

ROUTES

Fifteen airlines use Aberdeen Airport, offering approximately 30 destinations which include London, Amsterdam, Paris, Orkney and Shetland. Due to the fact that the runway is shorter than other major airports, many of the larger planes commonly used for holiday flights do not use the airport. Travelling to Tenerife from Aberdeen requires a plane to land for refuelling midway through the journey, as the combined weight of the aeroplane and fuel requires a longer take-off area. However, flights to London, Paris and Amsterdam are used by people wishing to fly further afield on holiday, as the Aberdeen flight provides a connection to these airports where they can transfer to other available flights. This does mean that the cost of convenience is added to the price of holidays for the Aberdeen Airport traveller. Some package holidays are available direct from Aberdeen, mainly to the Spanish islands, Malta and more recently Italy.

Online booking of tickets means that travellers just have to appear at the airport with their booking reference number. There is no longer any need for tickets to be sent out by post to customers.

A new airline has recently postponed the launch of flights from Aberdeen to Oslo (Norway). A lack of bookings forced the launch to be postponed until March. Travelling further north in winter did not appeal to the Aberdeen public. It is hoped that Swedish people will visit Aberdeen more frequently. Like Norwegians, they may find the price of consumer goods in Aberdeen to be much lower than at home.

SECURITY

As with all UK airports, security in Aberdeen Airport has had to be tightened in recent years. The first phase of a £1.5 million development has resulted in a new security search area. New technology is used to scan luggage and track passengers in some airports. Gatwick airport requires passengers to have their photograph taken and the details put into a barcode which is attached to the passenger's boarding card. Before boarding, staff use a barcode reader to check the photograph against the passenger.

In 2004 Aberdeen airport security received bad publicity when a girl climbed over the high security fence and spent the night in an aircraft.

Lengthier check-in times means that extra facilities are required in airports. Aberdeen airport has a café and a bar. A shop selling newspapers and magazines exists, along with a specialist shop called Baxters selling their own famous brands of fine gourmet foods, soups and preserves. The duty free shop sells a wide range of whiskies, many of which are not available in the local shops. They appear to be competitive in price.

ACCESS

The airport is accessible from Aberdeen city by road and rail. Bus links are provided, with fares set at approximately £1.30 for a single journey. Unfortunately, not all buses are designed specifically for airport travel. Passengers with large amounts of bulky luggage find access difficult. Taxi fares are approximately £12 per journey.

Although the railway station is 'close' to the airport, passengers still need to take a taxi when arriving by train. A proposal has been made to investigate the launch of a new railway station at the airport. This will obviously be very expensive and there are plans to start lobbying the Scottish Executive for funding. Easier access would hopefully increase the number of people using the airport, and Aberdeen's economy would improve as a result.

FLIGHTS

Incoming flights to Aberdeen face a 10pm curfew, after which no flights can land. Local residents have protested for many years at the prospect of this curfew being extended. They claim the noise would be unbearable. Delayed flights may be forced to land at Glasgow and Edinburgh and passengers transferred by bus to Aberdeen. This adds to the costs for holiday companies, who may choose not to offer holidays from Aberdeen airport for this reason. Passengers may not like the fact that they have added inconvenience, especially if they are returning from holiday and have to go to work next day.

CUSTOMER SATISFACTION

Each year BAA interviews 70,000 passengers to gather their customers' opinions. On a rating of one to five (five being the highest), Aberdeen Airport received an overall rating of four in 2004. Lack of trolleys and congestion were the most common complaints.

QUESTIONS

You should note that although the following questions are based on the stimulus material, it does not contain all the information needed to provide suitable answers to all the questions. You will need to make use of knowledge you have acquired while studying the course.

Answer ALL the questions.

Marks

1 Identify the problems of Aberdeen Airport and its passengers. Use the following headings. (Please identify problems only, solutions will not be credited.) **10**

- operations
- marketing
- finance

2 Passengers are able to purchase tickets using the internet.

Describe the advantages of e-commerce for: **8**

(a) consumers

(b) organisations.

3 The airport underwent a £1.5 million refurbishment.

Describe three sources of finance available to organisations undertaking large scale developments. **6**

4 Baxters sell branded goods at Aberdeen Airport.

Describe the advantages of branding for a business and its customers. **4**

5 British Airports Authority is a public limited company.

(a) Explain how a public limited company is influenced by the following stakeholders: **6**

- shareholders
- employees
- lenders.

(b) Describe the interest which each of the above stakeholders would have in the published accounts produced by the plc. **3**

6 BAA carry out interviews, using questionnaires, to assess customer satisfaction.

(a) Describe three other methods of field research which organisations may use to gather information. **6**

Marks

(*b*) Explain why market research does not always guarantee success in the market place. **4**

7 Explain what is meant by the term 'quality assurance' and describe the benefits it offers consumers of goods and services. **3**

(50)

C A S E   S T U D Y   5

Cashmere

This section should take you approximately one hour and 15 minutes.

Read through the following information, then answer the questions which follow.

CASHMERE IN BATTLE TO RETAIN ITS WORLD LEAD

Cashmere is a wool fibre produced traditionally in China, Mongolia and Iran from the under-hair of mountain goats. It is one of the rarest natural fibres, and is still hand-combed. It is also produced in Scotland. In 1985 several Scottish farmers recognised the benefits of introducing cashmere-producing goats to their farms. Financial support was given from groups such as Scottish Enterprise, Highland and Islands Enterprise and the European Commission to help the farmers form the Scottish Cashmere Producers Association. The Association aims to provide advice and assistance to new farms, and a central marketing operation for the collection and marketing of the cashmere fibre and products.

KNOWLEDGE AND SKILL

Presently in Scotland over 50 farmers with about 2,500 goats are producing fibre. This industry has benefited areas where alternative forms of farming have gone into decline. The aim is to build up the Scottish herd to at least 10,000 goats. The hills and upland landscape of Scotland suit goat farming.

Scotland is fortunate in that there are people in the country who have the necessary knowledge and skills in the specialised area of wool production. They are able to process the fibre into a luxurious and exclusive range of 100 per cent pure Scottish cashmere knitted goods. The packaging and a distinctive logo ensure that Scottish cashmere retains its exclusive identity. Ninety per cent of Scottish output is exported.

Case Study continues over the page

EXPORT PROBLEMS

The industry has not been without its problems. One of its main markets, the USA, imposed sanctions on imports of cashmere in what was referred to as the 'banana war'. The European Union entered into an argument with the USA over the purchase of bananas from the Caribbean, and the USA decided to retaliate by setting high price tariffs on many European items. The Scottish industry received some negative media coverage when it was reported that the Government used £30 million of aid to protect cashmere, when English organisations also affected by the trade embargo were not compensated. One press article suggested it was no coincidence that it happened at the same time as the Scottish parliamentary elections.

LUXURY FASHION

Cashmere is an expensive product. One hundred per cent cashmere scarves are sold online for approximately £35–45. Man-made scarves sell in street markets for a tenth of the price. Visitors to one of the newer members of the European countries, Czech Republic, can find cashmere and silk-mix scarves selling for £7.

Changes in fashion affect demand. Knitted products once considered to be 'old-fashioned' are now being shown by famous fashion designers in their catwalk shows, and are seen as 'cool' by the younger generation. Pringle Scotland has reported a massive increase in annual business. Famous people such as Robbie Williams, Madonna, David Beckham and Jamie Oliver have been photographed wearing Pringle jumpers. The company has shifted its target market into high value, high fashion areas and promotes it product as a luxurious brand. The label was shown at London Fashion week which is regarded as an important window for the fashion industry. The 'Cashmere made in Scotland' label is a quality symbol. Scottish cashmere is now seen as the best in the world.

CAREER PROBLEMS

Cashmere made in Scotland

The Scottish Cashmere Club strives to maintain the export success in cashmere while securing many thousands of jobs. Many jobs in other sectors of the Scottish knitwear industry have been lost in the past. The Borders of Scotland have been badly affected by job losses in this industry. Many of the large department stores, looking for cheaper products, found they could obtain them abroad where the wage rates are much lower. Lack of demand and the production of cheaper, easier to wash fabrics, were also contributory factors.

Younger people are also no longer interested in joining traditional industries when they embark upon their careers. The service sector jobs have greater appeal. A schools programme has been set up by Scottish Textiles and Careers Scotland to enhance the image of the textile industry. An industry which once shed 10,000 jobs in 12 months offers few prospects for school leavers or graduates. However, if the industry is to recover, the shortage of skills both at employee and management level must be resolved. The increased interest in Scottish Cashmere has made recruitment a priority.

FUTURE CHALLENGES

More recently, the World Trade Organisation has abolished quota protection, opening up the market. It is feared that Scotland will be under threat, as imports from countries such as China, Vietnam and India will no longer be restricted.

Chinese manufacturers, with easy access to the leading source of cashmere fibre in Inner Mongolia and the advantages of a low wage workforce, have built up the technology and skills to challenge the Scottish product.

Marketing and promotional campaigns have been used to reposition Scottish cashmere at the top end of the market.

Source: ***www.business.scotsman.com***

QUESTIONS

You should note that although the following questions are based on the stimulus material, it does not contain all the information needed to provide suitable answers to all the questions. You will need to make use of knowledge you have acquired while studying the course.

Answer ALL the questions.

Marks

1 Identify the problems faced in the Scottish Cashmere industry. Use the following headings. (Please identify problems only, solutions will not be credited.) **10**

- human resources
- operations
- marketing
- external

2 Financial support from external sources was made available to cashmere producers.

(a) Describe the costs and benefits of using external finance when establishing a new business venture. **5**

(b) Describe the types of non-financial support which are available to businesses. **3**

3 Wool production is a specialised process and requires skilled staff.

(a) Explain the costs and benefits of an in-house training programme introduced to increase the skill level of its employees. **5**

(b) Describe the contents and purpose of a job description in ensuring that the correct employees are appointed during a recruitment process. **3**

4 Trade sanctions are one example of an external influence on an organisation.

Describe two other economic influences which affect the running of a business. **4**

5 Cashmere products carry a quality symbol label.

(a) Describe the benefits of holding a quality symbol label for a manufacturer and their consumers. **5**

(b) Explain the benefits of using famous celebrities to endorse branded products. **3**

6 Potential consumers require information prior to purchasing products.

Describe the advantages and disadvantages of using: **6**

(a) written information

(b) oral information

when advertising a product.

7 Scottish Cashmere is seen worldwide as a quality product, and competitors may choose to use it as a benchmark.

(a) Describe what is meant by 'benchmarking'. **3**

Quality products may be marketed towards one particular market segment (such as AB grouping).

(b) Discuss the benefits of concentrating marketing efforts on one particular group of the market. **3**

(50)

Shipbuilding

This section should take you approximately one hour and 15 minutes.

Read through the following information, then answer the questions which follow.

There has been mixed news for shipbuilding on the Clyde in recent months.

THE GOOD NEWS

The good news is that more than £22.5 million is to be invested to create 401 new jobs and safeguard 205 existing jobs on the Clyde.

The money from BAE Systems and government regional selective assistance (RSA) will be ploughed into BAE's Govan and Scotstoun yards in Glasgow.

The plans were announced by Enterprise Minister Nicol Stephen.

He said that the investment was designed to improve the longer term competitive position of the yards across a range of naval work:

> 'BAE Systems' Glasgow yards have a tradition of excellence in marine engineering. I welcome the company's commitment to the future of the yards and to their workforce. I am delighted that we can play a part in helping to grow the business here through an RSA offer of £4.1 million.
>
> This will help to create 400 high quality manufacturing jobs and sustain more than 200 existing posts.'

BAE Systems has invested £30 million in the yard over the last five years. It will now invest more than £18m, along with the RSA funds.

Vic Emery, managing director of BAE Systems Naval Ships, said:

> 'The investments that we are making in our facilities on the Clyde, with the financial support of the Scottish Executive, will make us more competitive and better positioned to win future naval contracts, both for the UK and export customers.

We are proud of our long heritage in shipbuilding on the Clyde and confident for our future.'

'UPS AND DOWNS'

Mr Emery said that the yard had a number of contracts, giving a bright medium-term outlook, but there was more work needed for the longer term.

He added:

> 'Because of the ups and downs in our business, we need a better planned approach to our future work. That needs to come from a joining together of all of the shipyards around the country and also the defence procurement agency of the Ministry of Defence.'

BAE Systems Naval Ships has facilities in Scotstoun and Govan and in Filton, near Bristol. The company employs about 3,000 people and had a turnover of approximately £350 million in 2004.

Shipbuilding on the Clyde has been in a precarious state since the major closures in the 1980s and 90s. Cheaper production in the Far East, a reputation for delays, together with de-nationalisation all proved too much for what was once a major employer for both the upper and lower reaches of the river.

Tens of thousands of highly skilled workers lost their jobs, and now many of the skills needed are in short supply.

THE BAD NEWS

Further down the river in Port Glasgow, the news is less than good.

A Polish shipyard has beaten a Scottish rival in the contest for two public sector orders, it has been confirmed. The Remontowa yard in Poland has been named as the preferred bidder for a fisheries protection vessel ahead of Port Glasgow's Ferguson yard. The Gdansk yard has also won a contract to build a new ferry for use on Caledonian MacBrayne's Wemyss Bay to Rothesay route.

The bids were bogged down in a row over European competition regulations. Politicians queried the Scottish Executive's insistence that shipyards outside the UK had to be given the chance to tender for the work. Ferguson management and the Scottish National Party complained that Remontowa was using subsidies to undercut other submissions.

Managing director Richard Deane described the announcement as a setback but said the business, which employs about 300 people, was determined to carry on for the foreseeable future:

'We now want to put this behind us. We are resilient enough to work on other projects and we hope we will be successful on one or more of those in the coming months. We're not frightened of the future and we are resilient enough to bounce back from a setback. I wouldn't say that the shipyard is strong in business terms but the owners of the company are determined that we will remain as shipbuilders. They are backing their hopes for the future with their money, so we see no reason why we will not be trading and building ships for the foreseeable future.'

Environment Minister Ross Finnie said ministers were 'acutely aware' of the difficulties facing the Ferguson group, which may now have to make workers redundant.

The executive is issuing tenders for two other vessels, and he said he hoped that Ferguson would be able to bid successfully for at least one of them.

'BEST VALUE'

CalMac technical director John Kerr said value for money, reliability and delivery were the key factors in awarding the ferry contract to the Remontowa yard.

'There were four bids for the project in the end, and the Remontowa option clearly offered the best value for the investment', he said.

The Remontowa yard will build the second new vessel to serve the Wemyss Bay to Rothesay route – carrying 60 cars and 450 passengers – at a cost of approximately £9.5 million.

The executive's plans to build another Jura class fisheries protection vessel have been postponed, with tenders now being sought for an inshore Minna class vessel instead.

It was also announced that bids were being invited to build a ferry for Calmac's Largs to Cumbrae route.

Source: *BBC News*, 4 and 30 August 2005

QUESTIONS

You should note that although the following questions are based on the stimulus material, it does not contain all the information needed to provide suitable answers to all the questions. You will need to make use of knowledge you have acquired while studying the course.

Answer ALL the questions.

		Marks
1	Identify the problems faced by shipbuilding on the Clyde, both past and present. Use the following headings. (Please identify problems only, solutions will not be credited.) • external • operations • human resources • finance	**10**
2	Shipbuilding is large scale job production.	
	(a) Explain why job production is most suitable for shipbuilding.	**4**
	(b) Discuss the advantages and disadvantages of: • batch production • job production.	**6**
3	BAE Systems received government regional selective assistance to invest in the Scotstoun yard.	
	(a) Explain why the government may decide to give money to a business.	**2**
	(b) Identify and justify two other sources of finance for an organisation.	**4**
4	The government is a stakeholder in the Clyde shipyards.	
	(a) Discuss the influence of other stakeholders for an organisation.	**6**
	(b) Describe external factors that may affect the success of an organisation.	**5**

5 Shipbuilders need to keep tight control over their spending to ensure that costs do not rise.

(a) Explain the role of budgets for an organisation. **5**

(b) Outline how ratio analysis can also help to ensure that an organisation meets its objectives. **5**

(c) Describe the main elements of the final accounts of an organisation. **3**

(50)

Baxters Foods

This section should take you approximately one hour and 15 minutes.

Read through the following information, then answer the questions which follow.

George Baxter began his working life as one of more than 50 gardeners at Gordon Castle, but like so many Victorian Scots of even the most humble origins, he was blessed with an abundant spirit of enterprise. The Baxters story begins in 1868 when, with a little encouragement, he borrowed £100 from an uncle and other relatives and opened a small grocery shop in Fochabers.

Cleverly blending old ideas with new, and drawing on the abundance of fine local produce, his wife created an exceptional range of soups. She also pioneered the canning of soft fruit at a time when the whole process of canning was still very much in its infancy.

DEVELOPING THE BRAND

At the end of the Second World War, descendants of George Baxter, Gordon and his brother, Ian, came home to join the family firm. They found themselves in a business which had scraped through the bleak years of 1939 to 1945 by making and selling a little jam and not much else. Baxters then employed only eleven people, and its turnover in 1946 amounted to a mere £40,000 per annum.

All the while Gordon was feeling the growing urge to travel, to take his fine Scottish products abroad. Finally, in 1959, laden down with samples of jam and marmalade, he set off for the United States.

What he discovered on that and subsequent trips was to change the shape of the business in Fochabers forever. In America, people were instantly receptive to new ideas, business was refreshingly informal, and the commercial risks and rewards were immense. There – most importantly of all – he found a new and unfamiliar concept called 'marketing'.

Case Study continues over the page

CASE STUDIES

NEW IDEAS

Gordon returned to Scotland bursting with ideas. Uppermost of these was the revolutionary notion that you should not just sell what you made, but that you should find out what your customers want, then make it and then advertise it to them. He also decided to try out in Baxters a similar system to American companies, where independent directors sat on boards of large companies. Thus began the first ever appointments of non-executive directors to the Board of the family-owned business.

Throughout the 1960s and 1970s, Gordon and his wife Ena visited America so frequently that they came to be regarded as quasi-ambassadors for Scotland. No British food promotion in New York, Chicago, Los Angeles or Dallas was complete without the Baxter shop, often as the centrepiece. Ena's cooking demonstrations were seen by millions of American television viewers. She and Gordon hosted mammoth Scottish charity banquets, complete with pipers, singers and an all-Baxter menu.

CONTINUED GROWTH

The 1980s saw the business growing. Baxters traditional soups were already well established as the leading premium brand in the UK. Baxters beetroot and marmalade now also reached the number one position in their respective UK markets. During the course of the decade, the company's annual turnover tripled, from £10 million to over £30 million.

During this time, consumer tastes were also changing rapidly. A new health consciousness was beginning to emerge, along with a growing demand for different and more exotic flavours. The development team responded by introducing the highly successful Luxury, Special Occasion and Vegetarian soup ranges. Where possible, additives, preservatives and artificial colouring were completely eliminated and more emphasis placed on low-fat, high-fibre recipes. Higher-fruit, lower sugar jams began to prove extremely popular.

GROWTH AND ACQUISITION

A new state-of-the-art factory was opened at Grimsby in early 2001 which now produces the popular range of Baxters fresh soups. Also in 2001, Audrey Baxter (current Chairman of the company) and her team acquired Garner's Foods Ltd, owner of Garner's pickles, chutneys and salad dressings. That business continues to be run from its premises in Pershore, Worcestershire, where the Baxters' experience, knowledge, resources and passion is now ensuring that Garner's continues to achieve its fullest potential.

A second acquisition took place in 2003 when Baxters acquired CCL Foods plc based in Earls Colne, near Colchester in Essex. Baxters has now expanded its range of premium brands and private label business in the UK to include condiments and pickles under some of the UK's best-known brands, such as PizzaExpress, Peppadew, Simply Delicious, Olivaise and Mary Berry.

In September 2004, Baxters made their third acquisition with the purchase of Canada's leading private label soup manufacturer, SoupExperts Inc., providing them with the opportunity to grow the Baxters brand in the region. Based in St Hyacinthe in the Provence of Quebec, SoupExperts operate as a wholly owned subsidiary of Baxters Canada Inc. and, in addition to retaining the well-established private label business, will produce Baxters branded soups for the North American market.

Today, the Baxters brand continues to grow and develop.

Adapted from *www.baxters.co.uk*

QUESTIONS

You should note that although the following questions are based on the stimulus material, it does not contain all the information needed to provide suitable answers to all the questions. You will need to make use of knowledge you have acquired while studying the course.

Answer ALL the questions.

Marks

1 Identify the problems faced by Baxters. Use the following headings. (Please identify problems only, solutions will not be credited.) **10**

- marketing
- operations
- corporate management
- external

2 George Baxter could be described as an early entrepreneur.

(a) Define the term 'entrepreneur'. **2**

(b) Describe four qualities that contribute to becoming a successful entrepreneur. **4**

3 Gordon Baxter used his experience of marketing in the United States to influence the approach taken at Baxters.

(a) Explain how the theories of marketing concepts and the marketing mix can be combined to contribute to the success of products. **8**

(b) Describe the importance of market research to a company such as Baxters. **4**

4 Explain the purpose of the role of non-executive director in an organisation. **3**

5 Many modern companies choose to re-invest profits in their operations rather than use other sources of finance.

(a) Identify three other possible sources of finance available to a company such as Baxters. **3**

(b) Explain the benefits of using one of the sources of finance identified in (a) above. **2**

Marks

6 Baxters has grown through sustained acquisition (takeover).

(*a*) Explain the following terms:

- horizontal integration
- vertical integration
- diversification
- merger. **8**

(*b*) Explain why a company such as Baxters may prefer to grow by acquisition rather than by another method of growth. **2**

7 Baxters were revolutionary in their approach to producing canned products.

(*a*) Explain the term 'production system'. **2**

(*b*) Explain why quality control is essential to the success of a company such as Baxters. **2**

(50)

CASE STUDY 8

DC Thomson

This section should take you approximately one hour and 15 minutes.

Read through the following information, then answer the questions which follow.

BEANO BOYS RACE INTO PC GAME

The DC Thomson publishing empire was built on comics. The newspapers offered by the Dundee Company (such as *The Sunday Post* and *Dundee Courier*) have always been an important part of the business, but they never managed to match the 200 million copies of comics sold each year.

In the late 1950s, two comics, *The Dandy* and *The Beano*, sold more than two million copies together on a weekly basis. DC Thomson also published other successful comics – *Adventure*, *The Rover*, *The Wizard*, *The Skipper* and *The Hotspur,* some of which had served the children's comic market from the 1920s. The average child in the period between 1930 and 1960 read these cartoon comics avidly. Brand loyalty was established from an early age.

Tastes have now changed, and The *Beano* and *Dandy* have to compete with alternative characters such as Bob the Builder and Postman Pat. Recent figures have shown the sales of *The Dandy* and *The Beano* as having dropped considerably in the past 40 years. Despite the low price of 65p, sales are heavily dependent on free gifts attached to the cover.

A decision has been taken to allow the comic characters to be licensed and used in a computer game called Beanotown Racing. This is also to be developed for use with a Playstation 2. The computer game is being developed by a Dundee-based computer company and aims to build on the existing Beanotown website. Up until now, there has been a reluctance to allow the characters to be used for merchandising, which has been recognised as a missed business opportunity.

Other business ventures have included successful book sales (annuals), videos, clothing and confectionery. However, the management realise that in a market where millions can easily be spent on developing new brands or relaunching new ones, as happened with The Pink Panther and Thunderbirds, financial risk is never far away. Therefore DC Thomson's approach to brand building is a conservative one. Despite annual turnover rising, profits have dropped, as with the rest of the newspaper and magazine market. A need has been identified to generate additional revenue.

A cross-promotional campaign was launched with McDonald's Happy Meal. Although successful as a marketing technique, McDonald's' links with other organisations are always on a short-term basis as they aim to keep up the latest 'craze' being enjoyed by young people.

CHANGES FOR THE DANDY

In 2004 it was decided to redesign *The Dandy* in order to appeal more to today's 7–11-year-olds. Competition exists in the form of television and computer games. It was felt that the 70-year-old comic had become rather boring. The very first edition of *The Dandy* gave a free tin whistle; a 2004 edition offered a plastic tongue. The suggestion was made to the readers to serve a ham sandwich with the tongue hanging out. This was an attempt to maintain the 'wicked schoolboy" humour portrayed by the cartoon characters.

One of the comic characters, Desperate Dan, has also faced a makeover. Previously he carried a cowboy's gun, which had to be removed in light of the current political climate. Eating 'Cow Pie' was another of his famous traits. This had to be played down and his fat body slimmed to meet the current trend towards healthier eating.

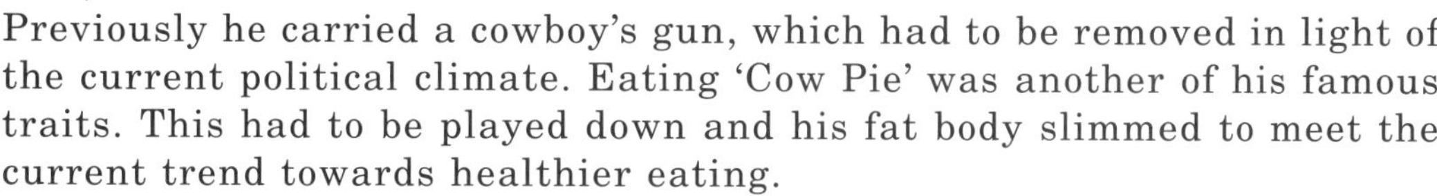

The quality of the paper used for printing also had to be improved, as the original comic was issued on newsprint. Newsprint allows a cheaper product to be produced but one which is not so nice to handle as glossier magazines. To ensure strict quality control of newspaper and comic production, DC Thomson installed the leading-edge digital Dotmeter. This huge investment in new technology was done in order to allow production of consistent high quality papers. Training in Germany was required to operate the equipment, again adding to costs.

Case Study continues over the page

CASE STUDIES

FACING THE FUTURE

The company does have a diverse portfolio of interests – comics, newspapers, investments in Scottish Radio Holdings, HIT Entertainment. The returns from these investments have not proved very successful. HIT Entertainment is the company behind Bob the Builder, seen as competition to some of DC Thomson's own comic characters.

Like other media companies, DC Thomson faces the problem of other companies reducing the amount of advertising due to their own need to cut costs. Financially DC Thomson has concerns, and at one point deferred payments into the salary pension scheme offered to its employees. Employees will be aware of other organisations who have failed to meet their pensions when they reach retirement age.

Market research showed that half of DC Thomson's readers were over the age of 55. There is a recognised need to attract a younger audience.

Business analysts state that DC Thomson need to embrace innovation and change more rapidly if it is to progress into the future.

DISTRIBUTION

Newspapers in Scotland are distributed by a wholesaler, WH Smith. They deliver papers to newsagents and supermarkets. Ideally consumers would place firm orders for a magazine and receive the magazine on a regular basis. Having magazines on supermarket shelves allows potential consumers to flick through the pages prior to purchasing. However, many magazines are returned to the shelf without a purchase being made.

Source: *www.scotsman.com, www.sundayherald.com*

QUESTIONS

You should note that although the following questions are based on the stimulus material, it does not contain all the information needed to provide suitable answers to all the questions. You will need to make use of knowledge you have acquired while studying the course.

Answer ALL the questions.

		Marks
1	Identify the problems faced by DC Thomson and the sale of comics in particular. Use the following headings. (Please identify problems only, solutions will not be credited.) • marketing • operations • finance	**10**
2	Compare the promotional methods which could be used by a magazine or newspaper publisher to encourage customers to: *(a)* place a regular order to a magazine each week *(b)* try a magazine for the first time.	**5**
3	The marketing of a computer game and website has been possible due to developments in ICT.	
	(a) Discuss how ICT could also be used to improve the operations process.	**5**
	(b) Describe two other methods of extending a product life cycle.	**2**
4	DC Thomson has invested money in other companies.	
	(a) Describe how the return on such financial investments can be measured using ratios.	**2**
	(b) Explain why this type of investment should not be judged on one year's ratio results alone.	**2**
	Investment by individuals or companies is a source of finance.	
	(c) Compare this source with two alternative means of funding.	**4**
5	DC Thomson's employees may be concerned about their pension entitlement.	
	(a) Explain the interests of stakeholders, other than employees, in an organisation's performance.	**4**
	(b) Describe the steps which an individual employee can take when she/he has concerns about their future within an organisation.	**4**

Marks

6 The introduction of a new printing technique has involved training in Germany.

(a) Describe the costs and benefits of attending a training course which takes place away from the normal workplace. **5**

(b) Explain how the organisation could measure the value of such a training course. **3**

7 An opportunity exists for DC Thomson to organise its business activities by product, such as comics, newspapers and linked merchandise.

Explain the costs and benefits of this type of structural organisation. **4**

(50)

CASE STUDY 9

Tilly Confectionery

This section should take you approximately one hour and 15 minutes.

Read through the following information, then answer the questions which follow.

Perhaps not the healthiest of foods but definitely one of Scotland's best-loved treats, tablet is set to capture a new generation of fans after being snapped up by Tesco, the UK's leading supermarket.

The small family firm, Tilly Confectionery, has won an order to put its handmade tablet on to the shelves of 48 of Tesco's stores throughout Scotland.

Clackmannanshire-based Tilly Confectionery, which also makes traditional sweets such as fudge, macaroon and coconut ice, currently sells about two tonnes of tablet a week, with an annual turnover of around £340,000.

THE TESCO DEAL

The Tesco deal will mean an increase in sales of £120,000 per year and, in addition, the company expects to increase the size of its workforce from 14 to 20 to meet the demand created by Tesco's order.

Peter Patterson started the company eight years ago, with his wife, Elisabeth, making the tablet in their kitchen. He says that the traditional style of the product, which is handmade without additives and preservatives, gives a real alternative to the mass-produced confections from multi-national companies normally found on supermarket shelves.

> 'People love the homemade taste and appreciate the quality of our ingredients and the care with which the tablet is made. We are absolutely delighted that more people will now have the chance to try it.'

Case Study continues over the page

HELP FROM SCOTTISH ENTERPRISE

The company has been helped to reach this pivotal stage in its development with support from Scottish Enterprise and Scottish Food & Drink. Maggie McGinlay, director of Food & Drink at Scottish Enterprise Grampian, states:

> 'Through the combined efforts of the industry, Scottish Enterprise and our partners, Scottish Food & Drink have developed a range of initiatives to help Scottish food and drink businesses achieve profitable and sustainable growth.
>
> This is a fantastic example of how a small company with a niche product and plenty of determination can get out into the market place and succeed.
>
> There is an increasing demand from consumers for locally-produced products to be available in supermarkets. We are trying to help more companies like Tilly supply that demand with a range of help and support, such as our Retailer/Supplier Excellence programme, which we hope will give these smaller companies a springboard to enable them to develop a consistent and profitable relationship with retailers in the future.'

Sarah Mackie, Tesco's senior buying manager, Scotland, said:

> 'Customers think that this tablet is delicious and really as good as homemade. We are delighted to add this, along with macaroon and fudge, to our range.
>
> It is yet another example of our commitment to ensuring that we have the right range for our customers in Scotland and are recognised as the natural Scottish retailer.'

Tesco believes that local sourcing effectively helps it grow its business because it satisfies local consumer needs and helps to build relationships with local suppliers. Tesco currently has 183 Scottish suppliers, with whom it annually invests about £676 million and lists over 1,000 regional lines.

SATISFYING LOCAL TASTES

However, most major supermarkets recognise the importance of local produce being available in their stores. Asda has a specialist local sourcing team whose focus is to satisfy the tastes and needs of local consumers. Based in Leeds, the team travels the country in search of local product ideas, listening to the views of customers and colleagues.

Like many specialist manufacturers, Tilly operates a website for selling many of their products online. Here they offer a range of gift baskets with a choice of products with mugs or soft toys, with prices between £20–30.

Due to the nature of their products, shelf life is limited to a maximum of six weeks from date of purchase. This is due to the lack of preservatives

and additives in their ingredients, which would normally enhance the life of the products. Tilly feel that this is what makes their products special and unique. They recommend that customers do not order too far in advance of when they need the product.

They accept credit card payment, which is handled by their secure credit card processing facility with Protx. All UK orders are delivered for £4.95, regardless of the size of the order.

They aim to dispatch orders the day after the order is received. Delivery times for UK deliveries are typically two to three working days from the date of placing of the order.

Adapted from *Scottish Food and Drink* website.

QUESTIONS

You should note that although the following questions are based on the stimulus material, it does not contain all the information needed to provide suitable answers to all the questions. You will need to make use of knowledge you have acquired while studying the course.

Answer ALL the questions.

		Marks
1	Identify the problems faced by Tilly. Use the following headings. (Please identify problems only, solutions will not be credited.) • marketing • operations • human resources • other	**10**
2	Tilly was able to win the new order with the help of Scottish Enterprise.	
	(a) Describe other sources of help and advice that are available to small businesses.	**4**
	(b) Explain the role of management in helping a business achieve its objectives.	**4**
3	Both Tesco and Tilly sell their products over the internet.	
	(a) Describe the advantages and disadvantages of e-commerce for the organisation.	**6**
	(b) Explain how ICT can be used effectively in other areas of the business.	**4**
4	Tilly does not make the baskets used in their gift packs.	
	(a) Explain the costs and benefits of outsourcing for an organisation.	**6**
	(b) Tilly is the brand name for the organisation's products, with the gift baskets being their premium product.	
	(i) Describe the benefits of holding a brand name.	**4**
	(ii) Explain how external factors can affect the success of premium products.	**5**

5 Tilly will now need to recruit new staff in order to meet the new order from Tesco.

(a) Describe the importance of staff training for a business to achieve its objectives. **4**

(b) Explain why some businesses are unwilling to invest money in training for existing employees. **3**

(50)

CASE STUDY 10

Thomson Holidays

This section should take you approximately one hour and 15 minutes.

Read through the following information, then answer the questions which follow.

INSIDE THOMSON

Thomson Holidays, a division of TUI UK Ltd, is part of the World of TUI. This is the largest tourism and services group in the world, employing 80,000 people in 500 companies worldwide.

The World of TUI is a world-class, innovative and customer-focused company which owns many of Europe's best known holiday brands and has leadership positions in its airline, inclusive tour business, and travel agency sectors. The group employs 17,500 people in the UK, Ireland, Sweden, Norway, Denmark and Finland.

Thomson Holidays is the market leader in the UK inclusive holiday market, a position it has held since 1974.

Thomson Holidays' head office is in London, but the majority of its 3,000 employees work overseas. The company has about one-third of the UK market, and operates to a wide range of resorts offering a variety of holiday types to suit all ages and tastes. All products and brands share the same philosophy – to be Number One, providing customers with the best possible holiday for their money.

AIRLINE

TUI Airlines incorporates Britannia Airways, one of the world's largest holiday airlines, offering award-winning service on a network of holiday flights from the UK and Europe to holiday destinations around the world. Britannia operates one of the most modern Boeing airline fleets in the world, with an average age of some five years.

Formed in 1962 and based at London Luton Airport, Britannia has a reputation for operational and technical excellence established over more than three decades. Throughout this period the airline has been a pioneer of modern aircraft types, fresh passenger service initiatives and new holiday destinations. In 2001, Britannia group of airlines will carry 9.5 million passengers to holiday destinations in over 100 countries worldwide.

REBRANDING

The now-famous 'smile' logo has already connected the Lunn Poly, Britannia and Thomson businesses for almost three years. As such it is a natural step to bring all these brands under the same name, Thomson.

More than 780 Lunn Poly holiday shops throughout the UK are being rebranded as Thomson. This change will also occur across high street travel agents, websites, holiday brochures, aircraft, call centres and television channel.

Peter Rothwell, Managing Director, TUI UK, said:

> 'Thomson is an extremely powerful brand in travel which has been known for high quality holidays since 1965. We need to maximise the brand. We want people to have a clear understanding that Thomson caters for all their travel needs, whether it's a one-way flight to Malaga, two nights at a city centre hotel in Paris, a villa in Italy or a five-star tailormade trip to Australia.'

Thomson's website has been upgraded to allow even more flexibility. People can book flights, holidays, hotel rooms, villas, apartments, spas and attractions anywhere in the world for any length of stay.

The company is also in the process of renaming its holiday airline from Britannia to Thomsonfly.

The company's Lunn Poly TV television shopping channel was also rebranded as Thomson TV at the end of 2005.

OTHER BUSINESS INTERESTS

The UK retail distribution businesses and channels within the World of TUI include:

Thomson: the UK's leading leisure travel retailer with over 750 retail stores, including the award-winning flagship Superstore, Thomson Direct call centre, and Thomson.co.uk where you can book and pay for holidays online. Thomson sells around 2.7 million holidays and flights per year, which accounts for over 20 per cent of the total market.

Team Lincoln: the UK's leading teletext and internet specialist, selling in excess of 250,000 holidays per year throughout the UK. It is based in the north east of England where it operates four call centres.

Callers Pegasus: one of the UK's leading regional retailers, also based in the north east of England. The company has approximately 20 shops, and a longstanding reputation for reliability, wide range of holidays and personal service.

Manchester Flights: the UK's leading and fastest growing teletext and internet specialist, selling in excess of 300,000 flights a year with a call centre operation based in Bury.

Also included is the management of TUI UK's state of the art Glasgow Call Centre. It sells close to a million holidays per year including Thomson Direct, Portland Direct, Founders Club and web sales.

Adapted from *www.thomson.co.uk*

Marks

QUESTIONS

You should note that although the following questions are based on the stimulus material, it does not contain all the information needed to provide suitable answers to all the questions. You will need to make use of knowledge you have acquired while studying the course.

Answer ALL the questions.

Marks

1 Identify the problems faced by Thomson. Use the following headings. (Please identify problems only, solutions will not be credited.) **10**

- human resources
- operations
- marketing
- other

2 Thomson is very customer-focused and aims to provide excellent customer service at all times.

(a) Explain how a business such as Thomson can use marketing as a means to attract customers and maintain its reputation. **6**

(b) Define the term 'market segmentation'. **2**

(c) Explain the importance of having an established market brand. **3**

3 Thomson has diversified into many other business areas.

(a) Explain why it may have adopted this strategy of growth. **4**

(b) Describe the terms 'horizontal and vertical integration', and explain why they may be a suitable method of growth for an organisation such as Thomson. **5**

4 Thomson is a large multinational company with employees in several continents.

(a) Describe the challenges faced by such an organisation in managing its workforce effectively. **4**

(b) Thomson also operates an airline. Staff training is essential in such a business.

Describe the methods of training and development that are likely to be adopted in keeping their staff up to date. **3**

(c) Identify and describe two forms of legislation which exist to protect employees. **4**

5 Financial control is important to every company operating in the Thomson group.

Describe the term 'budgets' and suggest why it would be important to use budgets in a business such as Thomson. **4**

6 The organisational culture in Thomson is centred around excellent customer service.

(a) Define the term 'organisational culture'. **2**

(b) Describe the likely roles and responsibilities of senior management in the operation of a multinational organisation such as Thomson. **3**

(50)

C A S E   S T U D Y   1 1

Scottish Whisky

This section should take you approximately one hour and 15 minutes.

Read through the following information, then answer the questions which follow.

THE SCOTTISH WHISKY INDUSTRY

One of Scotland's more famous industries, whisky, is hundreds of years old. The process of distilling barley and water results in the production of an alcoholic drink. The fact that the raw materials come from different geographical areas means that each brand retains an individual taste easily recognised by its consumers. Malt whiskies and blended whiskies exist. Single malts are whiskies produced in one single distillery; the cheaper blended whisky is a combination of different whiskies with cheaper grain products. Brand loyalty is strong. The products carry names emphasising the fact they are Scottish, such as Glenmorangie, Glenlivet and Glenfiddich.

Many brands are now owned by foreign companies, such as the French-based Pernod Ricard or Diaego. The takeover of another firm is a method of achieving growth.

THE UNITED STATES

Whisky sales in the US are increasing. Young people, living in New York, are seeing whisky as a 'cool' drink. The popularity has been created by a successful advertising campaign which has turned around the image of whisky, a drink once seen as being an appropriate drink for the older male population. Whisky is one ingredient of a cocktail which was awarded the title of International Cocktail of the Year 2004, and is now a popular choice in New York bars. Apparently the more expensive the whisky, the better the image with the young consumers. There is also a 'snob factor' of being able to identify the many different malt whiskies without reading the label. Premium pricing and strong imagery appeal to the young image-

conscious consumer. However, this is a market where tastes change very quickly. Presently, exporting whisky to the US is such a success that there are difficulties in obtaining sufficient stock. Firms have been forced to divert stocks destined for the European market to keep up with the demand.

However, the decline in the value of the US dollar means that Scottish exporters are taking a direct hit on profits, and their goods become more expensive to the American public. Prices may have to be increased. One owner reported an expected fall in profits of £100 million.

COMPETITION

The drinks market is a highly competitive one. Irish whiskey is a direct competitor to the Scottish brands, as are supermarkets' own labels. The increased consumption of beer and wine is also of concern to whisky producers.

WHYTE & MACKAY

In a brand-conscious market, not all the whisky companies have met with success. A South African entrepreneur took control of Whyte & Mackay when he purchased a German bank's 30 per cent stake. Reports stated that the bank sold the whisky producer for a loss. Bank of Scotland Corporate joined the entrepreneur, apparently taking over £135 million of debt. The new owners feel they can turn the company around in the long term by developing a portfolio of products. Whyte & Mackay faced difficulties in the past, one of which was their being involved in a cost-cutting war with a main competitor.

LABELLING

A pure malt whisky is one produced in a single distillery. Diageo was criticised for changing the composition of its Cardhu malt whisky to include malts from other distilleries, therefore they were not following the Scottish Whisky Association's guidelines. Cardhu was described as a 'pure malt' although it clearly was not.

Consumers may find the labelling and naming of whisky confusing. Blended whisky (a combination of malt and cheaper grain whiskies) was always marketed as a cheaper product to the more superior malt whisky.

A new term 'blended malted' meets the European legislation on labelling. The legislation will force some companies to alter their labelling in order to comply. Changing the label obviously involves additional costs.

THE HOME MARKET

The Scottish population has been identified by the Government as having high rates of health problems. Bad diet and excessive consumption of alcohol are named as contributory factors. Media coverage encourages consumers to change their habits. If successful, this will affect the profits of the drinks companies. Legislation may restrict marketing practices such as 'Happy Hours' where drinks are offered at low prices for a short period of time.

A large percentage of the price of Scottish whisky is paid to the Government in the form of taxation. This makes the product more expensive in the home market than abroad. Some people drive across the English Channel and purchase alcohol in large quantities. Supposedly for personal consumption, some of this is sold illegally, thus reducing the income of Scottish retailers. Pressure has been put on the Government to reduce tax over the years. The whisky industry adds great value to the Scottish economy in the form of export earnings and employment opportunities.

QUESTIONS

You should note that although the following questions are based on the stimulus material, it does not contain all the information needed to provide suitable answers to all the questions. You will need to make use of knowledge you have acquired while studying the course.

Answer ALL the questions.

		Marks
1	Identify the problems faced by the Scottish whisky industry. Use the following headings. (Please identify problems only, solutions will not be credited.) • marketing • operations • external	**10**
2	Producing good quality whisky depends on the combination of quality ingredients and a quality assured process.	
	(a) Describe the factors, other than quality, which influence the choice of a supplier of raw materials.	**4**
	(b) Explain how these factors might conflict with the need to obtain quality raw materials.	**2**
	(c) Describe the marketing benefits of having a quality assured process.	**3**
3	Justify an appropriate production method for a manufacturer of food and drinks products.	**3**
4	Branding is important in the whisky industry.	
	(a) Describe the importance of branded products with particular market segments.	**2**
	(b) Explain the measures which manufacturers of branded products can take to reduce the market share held by own label products.	**4**
5	A takeover is the purchase of one business by another, and is a means of growth.	
	(a) Describe the reasons for business growth.	**4**
	(b) Explain the effects of a takeover on the following stakeholders: • consumers • shareholders • employees.	**6**

6 Maintaining stock levels is essential in business.

(*a*) Describe the factors which influence the amount of stock held by a firm at any one time. **4**

At the end of each financial year, stock is valued and is shown on the organisation's balance sheet.

(*b*) Describe the contents and purpose of this financial statement. **4**

7 Whisky is sold by retailers such as supermarkets and specialist shops. It is also available online.

(*a*) Describe the advantages of using a retailer to distribute products. **2**

(*b*) Explain the additional benefits of using online retailers. **2**

(50)

C A S E   S T U D Y   1 2

Lingo24

This section should take you approximately one hour and 15 minutes.

Read through the following information, then answer the questions which follow.

The award-winning web-based translation service Lingo24 was founded in Aberdeen in September 2001, by Christian Arno following a successful pilot project with his friend and fellow Oxford graduate, Jos Shepherd. In August 2003, Lingo24 was named best e-business start-up in Scotland.

lingo24

OPERATING FOR 24 HOURS PER DAY

In November 2003 its New Zealand operation was set up with four employees. The clever thinking behind this was that when it is night here, it is daytime in New Zealand. This gave it the competitive advantage of operating for 24 hours per day. In a highly competitive industry, this meant that it could offer a very fast turnaround time. The company has grown rapidly, and now has additional operations in China and Romania.

With around 20 employees, Lingo24 has carved out a reputation as the translation company which goes where other translation companies fear to tread. Through innovation, flexibility and close interaction with their clients, they have successfully:

- met deadlines which other companies had declared impossible
- met budgets which other companies had declared impossible
- developed specially tailored services on request
- created client-focused software and workflow processes.

At the heart of their success is a passion for languages and technology. In April 2005 they recruited two long-standing partners, Jos Shepherd and Tom Sadler, to work full time in developing the company's technology.

The company offers a range of services including proofreading and checking, interpreting services, website localisation and internet marketing consultancy.

They have extensive experience in all areas, from technical translation to legal translation, and from creative copywriting in foreign languages, to documentation with very specific financial terminology.

CUSTOMER SATISFACTION

Lingo24 is now a leading brand in the provision of translation services. It can count companies like BP, Orange, Nissan, Honda, the Royal Bank of Scotland, the BBC, T-Mobile and MTV among their customers, with high levels of repeat business.

Customers have commented:

> 'Very impressed ... a fantastically customer-orientated service.'

CARING FOR THE ENVIRONMENT

Languages and technology are not their only passions. They take very seriously the impact of business on the environment and this is reflected in company policy and their operations. Lingo24 is concerned about sustainable development and has established an environmental policy for its employees worldwide to follow. All employees are aware of expected behaviour, and their website provides information so that other companies may see how simple it can be for them to help reduce their impact on the world's resources.

Their company policy insists that they make efficient use of energy, give consideration to the wider social and environmental implications of their actions at all times, and reduce the need for movement of both people and goods.

To achieve this, they promote environmental awareness among both employees and partners of Lingo24. They avoid unnecessary waste and encourage appropriate conservation, re-use and recycling. They consider their environmental performance as central to the overall business purpose, and review the performance annually.

In practical terms, their measures break down into three main areas:

- recycling
- workplace/home energy efficient measures
- travel policy.

Lingo24 is committed to the ongoing development of an environmentally responsible transport strategy. This strategy has two distinct elements: firstly, reducing the need for travel through advanced telecoms usage; and secondly, when travel is necessary, the use of the lowest impact means of transport possible.

To achieve this, all Lingo24 employees work from home, thus removing the need for daily travel to a place of work. It conducts the majority of its business by email and the telephone to reduce the requirement for travel. Where travel is required, journeys are planned to combine several meetings, in order to minimise the total amount of travel required.

Flying business class is banned within the UK except in exceptional circumstances and by prior agreement with management. Executives use the following means of transport in order of preference: foot, cycle, public transport, motor bicycle and private car. Sharing transport is actively encouraged.

Lingo24 staff use electronic formats wherever possible to cut down on paper usage.

Where printouts are required, they try where possible to use double-sided printing to reduce the weight of hard copy shipments.

However, other businesses have yet to sign up fully to supporting social responsibility.

Christian Arno reports:

> 'Finance has not been an issue because we have used our own cashflow to build the business, but it might have been if we'd tried to build it quicker. Banks will not lend to our business without a guarantee from the directors personally, because we do not have traditional assets on which they can secure the loan.'

QUESTIONS

You should note that although the following questions are based on the stimulus material, it does not contain all the information needed to provide suitable answers to all the questions. You will need to make use of knowledge you have acquired while studying the course.

Answer ALL the questions.

		Marks
1	Identify the problems faced by Lingo24. Use the following headings. (Please identify problems only, solutions will not be credited.) • marketing • operations • human resources • other	**10**
2	Good customer relations are very important to Lingo24's success.	
	(a) Describe the advantages and disadvantages of using a customer grouping.	**4**
	(b) Describe two other forms of grouping, and discuss the advantages and disadvantages of each.	**6**
3	Lingo24 currently has an entrepreneurial structure. As the business grows, it may have to change.	
	(a) Apart from size, explain the factors which influence the structure of a business.	**4**
	(b) Identify and describe the type of structure that Lingo24 may adopt in the future.	**4**
4	Lingo24 recruit new employees from around the world.	
	(a) Describe an effective recruitment process for Lingo24.	**5**
	(b) Explain how Lingo24 can ensure that they select the correct applicant for the job.	**3**
5	Lingo24 use job production.	
	(a) Compare the advantages of using job production with flow production.	**4**
	(b) Describe the quality factors that affect the operation of a business.	**4**

CASE STUDIES

6 Lingo24 are restricted in their growth due to the banks' unwillingness to lend because of their lack of traditional assets.

Apart from bank loans or mortgages, describe and justify sources of long-term finance available to a business. **6**

(50)

CASE STUDY 13

BAA

This section should take you approximately one hour and 15 minutes.

Read through the following information, then answer the questions which follow.

THE COMPANY

BAA is the world's leading airport company, at the heart of the world's transport network. Its airports are gateways to the cities and countries they serve. Not only did the company pioneer airport privatisation, retailing and security, it is widely recognised for its responsible and efficient airport operations.

BAA own and operate seven UK airports, through which hundreds of millions of passengers per year travel. Its success in UK airport management has allowed it to expand internationally, and it has management contracts or stakes in eleven airports outside the UK.

BAA is also a world-leading developer and manager of airport retailing. It is widely considered a world leader in airport security and was the first to introduce 100 per cent baggage screening for the hold. One-third of BAA staff work in security.

INVESTMENT FOR THE FUTURE

An average investment of £2 million per day on new airport facilities over the next decade, will support better, more efficient and more enjoyable travelling for millions of passengers. Nearly one in five of the world's international passengers travel through BAA's UK airports.

HIGH VOLUME BUSINESS

On average 1,651 aircraft depart from BAA's UK airports every day – approximately 103 per hour, one every 30 seconds. The 460-strong fire service is a key component of the airside team for maintaining a safe environment.

BAA's UK airports serve over 700 destinations and are used by around 300 airlines. BAA is dedicated to meeting customer needs, and every year BAA interviews approximately 70,000 passengers at its UK airports in its main survey of customer perceptions.

DEVELOPMENT

BAA is one of the UK's principal developers of infrastructure and one of the construction industry's largest clients, providing over 1 million square metres of commercial accommodation for more than 900 organisations at its airports. As such, BAA is also one of the largest commercial landlords in the UK, with a portfolio valued at £2 billion.

Its seven airports in the UK are: Heathrow, Gatwick, Stansted, Southampton, Glasgow, Edinburgh and Aberdeen. Its success in running UK airports has enabled it to take on the challenge of managing airports around the world. Outside the UK, BAA has management or retail contracts and stakes in airports in Australia, Italy and USA.

CORPORATE RESPONSIBILITY

BAA takes its social responsibilities seriously. It has a long and proud record of commitment to managing the environmental impacts of its airports and negotiating their growth with the communities directly affected. It aspires to be a leader among UK companies in the field of corporate responsibility.

BAA's success in running airports has led to expertise in other airport-related activities – property, retail, rail, construction, international airports, fire service, cargo, and safety and security.

The way in which BAA conducts business is as important as the results themselves. Integrity is the cornerstone of corporate responsibility and BAA expect everyone – directors, employees and suppliers acting on their behalf – to observe the highest standard of ethics.

COMMITMENTS

BAA makes the following commitments:

Safety and security: to provide a healthy and safe working environment by giving safety and security the highest priority at all times. BAA will systematically assess and manage its risks through audited best practice management systems.

People and leadership: to inspire people to excel through demonstrating the highest levels of personal performance, clear leadership and recognition of significant achievement. BAA will create an innovative environment that encourages teamwork, sharing and learning, open communication, and measurable performance improvement.

Customers, suppliers and business partners: to ensure that the services which BAA provides to its passengers and airlines are excellent and good value for money. BAA will work with its suppliers and business partners to measure and improve processes and services so that it creates added value for all concerned.

Shareholders: to encourage investors to believe in the company by giving shareholders strong continuous growth in earnings and dividends, and by generating the funds to grow our business.

Community and the environment: to work in partnership with local communities, setting challenging environmental targets and auditing performance against them.

Adapted from *www.baa.com*

CASE STUDIES

QUESTIONS

You should note that although the following questions are based on the stimulus material, it does not contain all the information needed to provide suitable answers to all the questions. You will need to make use of knowledge you have acquired while studying the course.

Answer ALL the questions.

		Marks
1	Identify the problems faced by BAA. Use the following headings. (Please identify problems only, solutions will not be credited.) • operations • human resources • corporate management • external	**10**
2	BAA aims to demonstrate corporate responsibility.	
	(a) Define the term 'corporate responsibility'.	**2**
	(b) Explain how a company such as BAA may be affected by external stakeholders who question its environmental record.	**4**
	(c) Identify three other stakeholders in BAA and explain the influence which they may exert over BAA.	**6**
3	BAA continues to make considerable investment in its airports.	
	(a) Describe two possible sources of finance available to fund this continued investment.	**2**
	(b) Explain how changes in the following areas may affect BAA's business operations: • environmental • political • economic.	**6**
4	BAA carries out frequent market research to find out what its customers think of its service.	
	Explain why this type of research is important, and describe how the business may react to the findings.	**5**
5	Explain the term 'span of control'.	**2**

6 BAA aims to create and maintain a safe working environment for its employees.

(a) Identify and describe two forms of legislation relating to the employment of staff. **4**

(b) Explain how the provisions of health and safety legislation might impact on an organisation such as BAA. **5**

(c) Explain how staff appraisal and staff development can work together to benefit both the organisation and its employees. **4**

(50)

CASE STUDY 14

Dairy Farmers

This section should take you approximately one hour and 15 minutes.

Read through the following information, then answer the questions which follow.

DAIRY FARMERS STAGE MILK PROTEST

Scottish dairy farmers have blockaded the country's major milk tanker depots in a protest over pricing policies.

During the second blockade in a fortnight, farmers targeted eight sites as part of the campaign for a fairer price for their milk. According to the National Farmers Union (NFU), one in four Scottish dairy farmers has gone out of business over the last six years. However, milk processors have insisted that they pay top prices.

John Kinnaird, president of NFU Scotland, said: 'There are only 1,400 dairy farmers left in Scotland and the industry is now at breaking point.' There were almost 5,000 producers about 20 years ago.

Ken Boyns, head of economics at the Milk Development Council, said that the UK retail average price for milk was about 52p a litre. In 2003 it was estimated that supermarkets made about 13p a litre, processors about 16p a litre and farmers 18p a litre. In 2004 the average UK milk price received by the farmer was 18.5p, but Mr Boyns pointed out that production costs vary across the country.

INCREASED PRICES – BUT NOT FOR THE FARMERS

While supermarkets, corner stores and those delivering milk to the doorsteps have increased the price of milk, most dairy farmers have seen very little of it, the NFU said.

Mr Kinnaird added: 'These family farms represented at protests today are being run out of business by companies that see no further than their next shareholder statement.'

However, a spokesman for Wiseman Dairies, which was targeted in the protests, said it paid its farmers 20.1p a litre:

> 'That is a long way from the 17p being quoted by farmers taking part in the protests.
>
> Our profit is 2p per litre with our figures for the last financial year showing 5 per cent profit, which is by no means excessive.'

The Scottish Consumer Council gave its backing to the farmers and called for discussions between all those involved. Its chairman, Graeme Millar, said:

> 'Many consumers are likely to be surprised to find that only around a third of what they pay for milk goes back to the farms that produce it.
>
> Farmers deserve a better deal, and milk processors should get together with retailers and the farmers to decide how this should best be done – without passing on any increased cost to consumers. It is in the interests of consumers that the marketplace works. If farmers are forced out of business, we may have to import milk and the price is likely to increase. No one wants to see that happen.'

SUPPORT FOR FARMERS' CASE

Dr Kevin Hawkins, of the British Retail Consortium, said that it is farmers who supply dairies not supermarkets, and processors and smaller retailers receive the money from price increases.

Scottish Green Party co-convener, Robin Harper, said:

> 'It is sad that the situation has come to this – but it is time to stand up for what is right and to demand fair trade for farmers.
>
> The continuing exploitation of dairy farmers by Tesco, Asda, Morrisons and Sainsbury's, and the milk processors is unacceptable. Processors cannot avoid responsibility.'

The Greens have called for a supermarket regulator to police the industry. The Scottish Tories agriculture spokesman, Alex Fergusson, said: 'Scottish Conservatives believe that the time has come to strengthen the existing Supermarket Code of Practice to give it real teeth, if necessary by new legislation.'

Sean Rickard from Cranfield University used to be the chief economist for the NFU. He said: 'We have too much milk, too many farmers producing too much milk, it's basically a commodity and as long as you are in that position, the price will always be weak.' He said that farmers should join together into co-operatives to process milk if they want a greater share of profits.

Co-operatives do exist, but farmers are unlikely to spend money in modernising their farms or investing in co-operatives if the future is so uncertain.

Dairy farmer John Cummings was taking part in a protest outside Robert Wiseman headquarters in East Kilbride. He insisted there was a shortage of milk in the UK this year. He added:

> 'The housewife is paying in the region of 55p and the farmer is getting 17p. We are sending a message to the supermarkets that if we do not get a substantial increase in the price of milk in the region of 4p, we are going to cut the supply of milk off across the whole country and you can go to Europe and get your milk if you want.'

A recent visit from the US to Yorkshire attracted a lot of interest from local dairy farmers. The team from South Dakota are trying to entice dairy farmers to move to the US where they are guaranteed higher prices for their product.

The UK is becoming more and more dependent on other countries to put food on the table. The latest figures show that Britain now produces 63 per cent of the food we eat, compared with 75 per cent ten years ago.

With threats to global security, some believe we are putting ourselves in danger by relying so heavily on imports.

QUESTIONS

You should note that although the following questions are based on the stimulus material, it does not contain all the information needed to provide suitable answers to all the questions. You will need to make use of knowledge you have acquired while studying the course.

Answer ALL the questions.

		Marks
1	Identify the problems faced by the Scottish milk industry. Use the following headings. (Please identify problems only, solutions will not be credited.) • marketing • operations • finance • human resources	**10**
2	Supermarkets have increased the price of milk sold to consumers, and milk is an example of a mass market product.	
	(a) Explain why price is an important part of the marketing mix.	**3**
	(b) (i) Distinguish between differentiated and undifferentiated marketing.	**2**
	(ii) Describe the advantages and disadvantages of market segmentation.	**4**
3	The information given to the milk industry is that there is currently too much milk being produced.	
	(a) (i) Describe the different types of information available to an organisation.	**4**
	(ii) Explain the importance of good quality information in decision-making.	**6**
	(b) Explain how an organisation can find out if a decision was effective.	**3**
4	'Scottish dairy farmers have blockaded the country's major milk tanker depots in a protest over pricing policies.'	
	(a) Identify and describe two forms of industrial action that employees could take when in dispute with their employers.	**6**
	(b) Describe the processes involved for an organisation and its employees to resolve industrial disputes.	**4**

CASE STUDIES

5 Some farmers formed producer co-operatives to sell their milk to the processors.

(a) Discuss the advantages and disadvantages of two other types of business organisation. **6**

(b) Describe the role of enterprise in the success of an organisation. **4**

(50)

CASE STUDY 15

McCowans Highland Toffee

This section should take you approximately one hour and 15 minutes.

Read through the following information, then answer the questions which follow.

A STICKY END FOR TOFFEE LEGEND?

McCowans Highland Toffee, with its famous Highland cow logo, has kept many a young mouth chewing since the 1920s. However, in March 2005, *The Mail on Sunday* reported the company as 'facing a sticky end' after receivers had been called in. One hundred jobs within the Stenhousemuir-based firm were at risk. The workforce was reassured that McCowans would continue to trade until a buyer was found who was willing to take on the business as a going concern. This caused uncertainty among the workforce.

The company has an established and strong brand name, and has strong positions in the chew bar and bonbon markets. Only recently the company was considering the possibility of additional investment, but trading conditions have proved difficult due to the increasing costs of raw materials. British manufacturers are paying over three times the world market price for sugar, one of the sweet confectioner's main ingredients. Many raw materials cost European manufacturers more than the global price due to trade protection schemes. Movements in the currency exchange rate have meant that the cost of importing raw materials has also increased for many manufacturers.

The company has already undergone internal restructuring to survive. Originally founded in the 1920s by Andrew McCowan, A McCowan & Sons Ltd was sold to Nestlé in the 1960s and was the subject of a management buyout in the late 1980s, before being bought by the Dutch company Phideas in the mid 1990s for £3 million. There was another management buyout in 2003.

In 2004, a £125,000 regional selective assistance grant was awarded for an expansion project. Sourcing finance is never easy for smaller organisations. Also in 2004 McCowans paid almost a seven figure sum to

buy out an English sub-contracting manufacture of its bonbon brand. This acquisition was facilitated by the Clydesdale Bank. Borrowing money is always risky as interest payments mean another expense to the organisation. This was done in an attempt to broaden the product base, and to deal directly with top-named customers like Cadbury, Asda and the Coop. The product is not always easy to find for the consumer, although small independent retailers seem to stock it. The purchase allowed them to acquire the plant and customer goodwill associated with the bonbon business. Such developments gave no hint of today's problems.

PRODUCT RANGE

McCowans make many products besides Highland Toffee. They produce a 'Toxic Waste' bar, a 'Streaker' bar, and have entered a deal with drinks manufacturer Vimto to produce a Vimto bar. The names of these products suggest that they are targeting the younger end of the confectionery market. Sweets (bonbons) meet the need of the older consumer. Many older customers find that McCowans products are nostalgic, bringing back childhood memories. Several websites show McCowans' and other products which are remembered by the older consumer as something they ate as a child. Five bars of McCowans Highland Toffee can be purchased for £2.49. The price is also quoted in US dollars. It is not possible to deal directly with McCowans online, a missed business opportunity perhaps. Search engines produce many web addresses, when McCowans Toffee is keyed in, ranging from toffee recipes to football clubs!

HEALTHY EATING

The company's shock entry into receivership was also reported in *The Scotsman*. They report that the confectionery market's future is uncertain because of healthy eating trends. Parents, pressurised by the media and more aware of the unhealthy diet of their children, restrict the amount of sweets which children consume. One Scottish model is suing the company for the cost of her dental treatment, claiming the acidity of the product damaged her teeth. If successful, this could snowball into further legal claims, costing the firm a great deal of money.

COMPETITION

Entering any sweet shop, it is easy to see the vast range of competitive products. Children like to try new products, and traditional toffee products may not meet the current trend. Cadbury and Walkers crisps market their products strongly on television and have been criticised for issuing vouchers allowing schools to obtain equipment. The Food Standards Agency has also cracked down on the marketing of sweets and snacks to children. Promotional pricing is used by the manufacturers and supermarkets to encourage increased consumption. It is difficult for smaller companies to compete with the marketing budgets of large companies such as Cadbury, who are reported to spend £10 million on promoting the soap opera 'Coronation Street' alone. Attractive websites where children can play games are also produced by these companies, which is yet another form of promotion.

Source: *The Mail on Sunday,* 5 March 2005; *www.news.scotsman.com; www.bbcnews.co.uk*

QUESTIONS

You should note that although the following questions are based on the stimulus material, it does not contain all the information needed to provide suitable answers to all the questions. You will need to make use of knowledge you have acquired while studying the course.

Answer ALL the questions.

		Marks
1	Identify the problems faced by McCowans and its employees. Use the following headings. (Please identify problems only, solutions will not be credited.) • operations • external factors • finance • marketing	**10**
2	The company has undergone internal restructuring. Describe what is meant by the term 'delayering' and discuss the benefits it offers to an organisation facing similar difficulties to McCowans. Diagrams should be used to support your answer.	**7**
3	Sourcing finance is never easy for smaller organisations. Describe three suitable sources of finance for the smaller organisation.	**6**
4	McCowans use a wholesaler to distribute their products. Describe the advantages and disadvantages of using the following channels of distribution: • wholesalers • retailers.	**7**
5	McCowans have numerous products within their product line.	
	(a) Explain the benefits of having an extensive product line.	**4**
	(b) Describe three suitable promotional methods which companies can employ when their advertising budget is much smaller than that of competitors.	**3**

6 McCowans has been the subject of takeover in the past.

Explain the reasons why firms take over other companies who produce similar products to their own. **5**

7 A manufacturing firm has to purchase raw materials.

(a) Explain the factors which influence a choice of supplier. **5**

(b) Discuss the benefits of employing a computerised stock control system. **3**

(50)

SECTION TWO

Exam Style Questions

Exam Style Questions

EXAM STYLE QUESTIONS

		Marks
1	Entrepreneurs take risks to set up in business, but can reap the rewards if successful.	
	(a) Describe the characteristics of a successful entrepreneur.	**4**
	(b) Describe the steps employed in using a decision-making model to reach a business decision.	**6**
	(c) (i) Identify two types of organisational structure.	**2**
	(ii) Describe the types of organisational structure that you have just identified. You may use diagrams to support your answer.	**5**
	(d) Marketing is an important element in any business.	
	(i) Explain the term 'niche marketing'.	**2**
	(ii) Explain the importance of market research and its costs and benefits.	**6**
		(25)
2	Supermarkets such as Sainsbury's operate in a very competitive market.	
	(a) For each element of marketing mix, describe two methods which an organisation could adopt in order to gain a competitive advantage.	**8**
	(b) An organisation may use random or quota sampling when carrying out market research.	
	(i) Discuss the benefits and drawbacks of using: • random sampling • quota sampling.	**4**
	(ii) Describe the main advantages of using field research over desk research.	**4**
	(c) (i) Explain how a website set up by the supermarket could help market research.	**4**
	(ii) Information held by the supermarkets would be covered by the Data Protection Act. Identify the basic principles that the supermarkets must follow under the Act.	**5**
		(25)

			Marks
3	*(a)*	The Coca-Cola company distributes its products worldwide (including Coke, Malvern Water, Rose's Lime Cordial).	
		Describe a suitable method of grouping business activities for such an organisation.	**5**
	(b)	Explain the reasons for marketing products under different brand names as opposed to one overall name.	**6**
	(c)	The Coca-Cola company chooses to outsource the bottling part of its production process.	
		(i) Describe the difficulties which can result from outsourcing.	**4**
		(ii) Describe the most appropriate production method for a manufacturer of soft drinks.	**4**
	(d)	(i) Discuss the reasons for marketing products which have remained at the maturity stage of the product life cycle.	**3**
		(ii) Explain three means by which a product life cycle can be extended.	**3**
			(25)

4		Business has an important role to play in modern society.	
	(a)	Describe the role of business in society, relating your answer to: • wealth creation • satisfaction of wants.	**4**
	(b)	The entrepreneur plays an important part in modern business.	
		Discuss the function of the entrepreneur in relation to: • combining factors of production • innovation • risk-taking.	**6**
	(c)	Explain why an organisation may feel pressurised into investing significant amounts of money in ICT.	**5**
	(d)	Current trends point towards greater flexibility in the working population.	
		(i) Explain why organisations may prefer to recruit staff on a temporary and part-time basis.	**5**
		(ii) Discuss the advantages to an organisation of using a recruitment agency.	**3**
		(iii) Identify two pieces of legislation relating to employment.	**2**
			(25)

Marks

5 Providing a quality service is important in the hotel industry, and customers can judge hotels by AA and RAC star ratings.

(a) Identify two other quality standards and discuss the benefits they bring to an organisation. **6**

(b) Large hotel chains operate in most of the major cities in the UK. Decision-making is carried out centrally.

Discuss the advantages and disadvantages of centralised decision-making. **6**

(c) Financial information is used by managers when making decisions.

(i) Justify the use of the following two ratios in decision-making: **4**

- net profit ratio
- rate of stock turnover.

(ii) Explain the limitations of using ratios as the only means of decision-making. **5**

(d) Describe how ICT can improve the operational function of a hotel. **4**

(25)

6 *(a)* Some large organisations have core staff, contractual staff and casual staff.

(i) Explain each of these terms. **3**

(ii) Discuss the advantages and disadvantages of employing contractual and casual staff. **5**

(b) Discuss the benefits of flexible working for both the employer and the employee. **5**

(c) Discuss the health and safety implications of employees working from home. **4**

(d) (i) Describe how improvements in ICT have made working from home a more acceptable option for the organisation. **4**

(ii) Describe the costs involved in using ICT in the workplace. **4**

(25)

			Marks
7	*(a)*	Some small firms choose to remain as sole traders. Describe two advantages and two disadvantages of being a sole trader.	**4**
	(b)	Employees are stakeholders who can have an important influence on the organisation. Identify three other stakeholders and describe how they can influence the organisation.	**6**
	(c)	(i) Discuss the factors that can affect the quality of a decision.	**5**
		(ii) Explain how a manager can find out if a decision was effective.	**4**
	(d)	The quality of materials will help an organisation decide which supplier to use. Describe other factors that a purchasing manager should consider when choosing a supplier.	**6**
			(25)

8	*(a)*	(i) Describe the factors which influence an organisation's type of structure, such as tall or flat.	**5**
		(ii) Discuss the effects of changing from a tall to a flat structure.	**3**
	(b)	In recent years, numerous football clubs have become public limited companies.	
		(i) Explain the reasons why organisations may choose to operate as public limited companies.	**4**
		(ii) Discuss the effects on ownership and control of becoming a plc.	**4**
	(c)	One football club, whose spectator numbers are falling, decides to implement new marketing techniques.	
		(i) Describe two suitable promotion methods which the football club may employ.	**4**
		(ii) Discuss how media coverage can affect the image of a football club.	**5**
			(25)

Marks

9 Multinational businesses such as Sony achieve success by continually updating their product portfolio.

(a) Explain why a good product mix would help a business to remain successful. **6**

[A diagram may be used to support your answer.]

(b) Sony depends on shops holding large amounts of stock. Describe the problems caused by: **6**

- overstocking
- understocking.

(c) Describe the actions which an organisation could take in order to prolong the life of one of its products. **6**

[A diagram may be used to support your answer.]

(d) Explain how the use of a SWOT analysis could be used to decide which products should remain in an organisation's product mix. **4**

(e) Explain the importance of the role of managers in decision-making. **3**

(25)

10 Many garden centres have added a café to their premises as a means of extending their business.

(a) Explain the reasons why an organisation may choose to increase the range of products which it offers. **4**

(b) Using a diagram, describe one method which may be used to extend the product life cycle. **3**

(c) Garden centres sometimes need to give advice to customers, and therefore wish to attract staff with a knowledge of gardening.

(i) Describe the document which would ensure that an applicant would know if the job was appropriate for them. **4**

(ii) Many organisations choose to train staff they have employed for many years. Explain the role of an appraisal interview in identifying training needs. **4**

(d) Businesses which serve food have to comply with the Health and Safety at Work Act.

(i) Describe how this Act affects both employees and employers within an organisation. **6**

(ii) Explain the means by which changes in legislation can affect an organisation. **4**

(25)

Marks

11 (*a*) Explain the following business objectives: **6**

- sales maximisation
- social responsibility
- profit maximisation.

(*b*) Discuss the advantages and disadvantages to an organisation of diversifying its product range rather than entering into a merger. **6**

(*c*) Business organisations depend on information.

(i) Identify and describe two sources of information. **4**

(ii) Describe the characteristics of good information. **5**

(*d*) Justify the use of SWOT analysis by managers in making decisions. **4**

(25)

12 All business organisations must carefully manage their finances in order to remain competitive and successful.

(*a*) (i) Explain the purpose of preparing a profit and loss account and a balance sheet. **6**

(ii) Explain the meaning of liquidity and why it is important for an organisation to manage its cashflow. **5**

(*b*) Identify and explain the purpose of two accounting ratios. **6**

(*c*) Many businesses use organisation charts to depict their structure.

(i) Explain the terms 'span of control' and 'organisation culture'. **4**

(ii) Describe the role and responsibilities of senior management within an organisation. **4**

(25)

Marks

13 Supermarkets have to hold large stocks of popular goods.

(a) (i) Discuss the advantages and disadvantages for organisations of holding large quantities of stock. **6**

(ii) Explain the effects of holding large amounts of stock on an organisation's cash budget. **2**

(b) Supermarkets offer both branded goods and own label goods.

Describe the advantages of selling **6**

- branded and
- own label goods

for the supermarket and its consumers.

(c) Explain the steps which a human resource manager should take when the organisation has a high staff turnover. **3**

(d) (i) Describe the means of selecting suitable staff for a supermarket. **5**

(ii) Suggest three measures which a human resource manager might take in order to retain high quality employees. **3**

(25)

14 Organisations in highly competitive markets need to be responsive to their customers' needs.

(a) (i) Explain the purpose of market research in meeting this objective. **4**

(ii) Describe three methods of field research that an organisation may use. **3**

(b) Some organisations may decide to form into customer groupings. Describe the advantages and disadvantages of grouping the organisation this way. **4**

(c) Selling over the internet – 'e-tailing' – has become very important to firms. Explain the advantages and disadvantages of internet-selling for: **8**

- the organisation
- the consumer.

(d) Most firms fail due to liquidity (cashflow) problems.

Identify possible sources of cashflow problems and describe one solution for each source you have identified. **6**

(25)

Marks

15 *(a)* ICT can be used in all the functional areas of the organisation. Describe how it could best be used in: **6**

(i) marketing

(ii) operations

(iii) finance.

(b) (i) Describe the actions which a business could take if it found that there had been a reduction in its profitability ratios. **3**

(ii) Explain how these actions may conflict with the business's other objectives. **3**

(c) (i) Discuss the advantages and disadvantages of using job production. **4**

(ii) Describe how mass manufacturers such as Dyson can ensure a high standard of quality in their production systems. **6**

(d) Describe the role that public relations plays when a manufacturer fails to achieve a high quality in its production. **3**

(25)

16 An organisation is considering introducing a new mechanised production process. On-the-job training will be provided for the staff.

(a) Describe off-the-job training and justify its use for the organisation. **4**

(b) Explain the benefits of staff training for an organisation and its workers. **6**

(c) A mechanised production process suggests that flow production is used. Discuss the advantages and disadvantages of: **8**

(i) flow production

(ii) job production.

(d) Manufacturing organisations regard it as important that they produce quality goods. Describe the means by which organisations can check that they produce quality goods at all times. **7**

(25)

EXAM STYLE QUESTIONS

Marks

17 Quality is central to the production of desirable goods and services.

(a) (i) Explain how a manufacturing organisation can ensure quality in the production process. **4**

(ii) Describe the benefits of: **5**

- benchmarking
- quality circles.

(b) (i) Describe the problems faced by organisations which use warehouse facilities for the storage and distribution of finished goods. **4**

(ii) Explain the importance of road transport as a means of delivery in the UK today. **3**

(c) Explain why an organisation may prefer to adopt a decentralised structure rather than a centralised structure. **5**

(d) The new finance director has indicated the need for the organisation to reduce and monitor costs.

Explain the use of budgets in monitoring and controlling costs. **4**

(25)

18 *(a)* Compare the characteristics of the following types of business organisation: **4**

- sole trader
- public limited company.

(b) (i) Describe one suitable source of finance for an entrepreneur wishing to start a new business as a sole trader. Justify your choice. **2**

(ii) Describe the advantages of franchising for a franchisee and franchisor. **5**

(c) Control of cashflow is vital for a sole trader's success. Explain five means by which cashflow problems can be resolved. **5**

(d) The sole trader is likely to employ an entrepreneurial form of organisation structure.

(i) Describe what you understand by the term 'entrepreneurial structure'. **2**

(ii) Explain the differences and similarities of hierarchical and flat structures. **7**

[Diagrams should be used to support your answer.]

(25)

Marks

19 When the supermarket Morrision's acquired Safeway, it ran into problems in merging the two businesses, which may take a number of years to sort out.

(a) Identify and describe this type of integration. **3**

(b) (i) Explain the internal factors that may have caused problems for Morrison's. **4**

(ii) Describe how a structured decision making model could help overcome these problems. **6**

(c) (i) Describe pricing strategies that could be employed by large supermarkets. **6**

(ii) Discuss which advertising media would be most suitable for their pricing strategies. **6**

(25)

20 All organisations need to monitor and control their financial position to ensure that they survive and are successful.

(a) (i) Describe two methods which ensure that the business remains liquid. **4**

(ii) Explain and justify three alternative sources of long-term finance which could be used by a firm taking over a rival. **6**

(b) (i) The efficient control of stock is essential for the liquidity of the organisation. Describe an effective form of stock control that could be used in a business. **6**

(ii) Some organisations have adopted a 'Just in Time' system of stock control. Explain the possible dangers of using this system for the organisation. **4**

(c) Explain the factors that the organisation should consider when deciding on a channel of distribution for its finished stock. **5**

(25)

EXAM STYLE QUESTIONS

Marks

21 Text messaging and email can be used by organisations to market products.

(a) (i) Describe the constraints facing organisations who wish to adopt these marketing methods. **4**

(ii) Explain how promotional tactics might enable organisations to increase the use of this marketing technique. **4**

(b) One objective of marketing is to improve the image of a business.

(i) Explain how an improved image might benefit the following stakeholders: **3**

- customers
- employees
- shareholders.

(ii) Identify three further objectives of an organisation and describe the involvement of the marketing department in ensuring that they are achieved. **6**

(c) When a marketing department wishes to develop a promotional idea, it is allocated a budget.

(i) Discuss the use of budgets as a management tool. **5**

(ii) Explain how the marketing and financial functional areas may face conflicts of interest within an organisation. **3**

(25)

22 *(a)* Explain, with examples, what is meant by each of the following types of decision: **6**

- strategic
- tactical
- operational.

(b) On finding that a strategic decision has not been carried out effectively throughout an organisation, communication problems are identified.

Explain how an intranet system could help to improve the situation. **4**

(c) (i) Describe two sources of information which could support the decision-making process. **2**

(ii) Compare the strengths and weaknesses of internal and external sources of information. **6**

(d) An organisation sets the objective of increasing profit. Explain the role of the following functional departments in achieving the objective: **7**

- marketing
- research and development.

(25)

Marks

23 Different businesses have different objectives, but they all seek to survive.

(a) (i) Identify and describe three types of business organisation. **6**

(ii) Explain the following business objectives: **6**

- profit maximisation
- sales maximisation
- social responsibility.

(b) Stakeholders can exert positive and negative influences on businesses.

Identify three stakeholders and describe the influences that they may have on an organisation. **6**

(c) Businesses depend on their employees and must maintain good working relations.

Discuss the processes available to an organisation and its employees when there is a breakdown in relations. **4**

(d) Describe the impact of equal opportunities legislation on an organisation. **3**

(25)

24 *(a)* Specialist training often takes place away from the workplace, and can be expensive.

(i) Apart from the expense, describe other costs involved in off-the-job training. **3**

(ii) Explain why training is important for the organisation to meet its objectives. **3**

(b) Well-trained staff can be used to promote the organisation's products. Describe other forms of promotion that the organisation can use with:

(i) the retailer **4**

(ii) the customer. **4**

(c) Explain why product development is important for businesses. **6**

(d) In order to find out what customers need in new products, the business should carry out market research. Describe the methods that could be used to gain this information. **5**

(25)

Marks

25 *(a)* (i) Describe the component parts of each of the following: **6**

- job description
- application form
- person specification.

(ii) Explain the difference between an aptitude test and a psychometric test, and justify the use of each of them. **6**

(b) Explain the impact on an organisation of the introduction of the following legislation: **6**

- Freedom of Information (Scotland) Act 2002
- Disability Discrimination Act 2005.

(c) (i) Explain how a company may benefit from exporting its products. **4**

(ii) Identify a source of assistance which may be available to an exporter. **1**

(iii) Distinguish between sales maximisation and profit maximisation. **2**

(25)

26 Organisations both consume and generate information.

(a) (i) Describe the difference between qualitative and quantitative information, and a use for each. **4**

(ii) Compare the costs and benefits of primary and secondary information. **5**

(b) Many organisations depend on and invest heavily in ICT.

(i) Identify three types of ICT used in modern business, and justify their use. **6**

(ii) Explain the impact of the Data Protection Act 1998 on business organisations. **4**

(c) Recruiting the best staff is essential to the success of every organisation.

(i) Explain the role of aptitude tests and psychometric tests in the recruitment and selection of new staff. **4**

(ii) Explain why an organisation may decide to use the services of a recruitment agency to source new staff. **2**

(25)

Marks

27 The media have suggested that there is interest in a takeover of one of the UK's largest department stores.

(a) (i) Explain the meaning of the term 'takeover'. **1**

(ii) Describe the consequences of a takeover for the following stakeholders: **6**

- shareholders
- customers
- employees.

(b) (i) Describe the means by which organisations can measure financial performance relative to previous years. **4**

(ii) Describe two other measures which need to be taken into account if the overall success of an organisation is to be measured. **3**

(c) A company which is losing market share needs to take steps to rectify the situation.

Discuss the promotional methods which would be effective in restoring market share. **5**

(d) Department stores need to be able to identify best-selling items in order to maintain appropriate stock levels.

(i) Explain how ICT can help an organisation to maintain appropriate stock levels. **6**

(ii) Describe the relevance of appropriate stock levels to a firm's success.

(25)

28 Quality is vital to the success of any organisation.

(a) Discuss the importance of quality inputs in operations. **4**

(b) (i) Describe the steps taken to ensure that the best quality staff are employed by the organisation. **8**

(ii) Explain how the quality of staff may be maintained after they join the organisation. **4**

(c) Describe the advantages and disadvantages of using an effective quality assurance system. **6**

(d) Identify and describe a quality standard used in organisations. **3**

(25)

Marks

29 Car manufacturers such as Volkswagen spend hundreds of millions of pounds on marketing their products every year.

(a) Explain, using examples, the benefits to an organisation such as Volkswagen of using: **5**

- pricing strategies
- promotional strategies.

(b) Volkswagen have started producing niche products such as the Eos coupe/convertible car.

Explain the term 'niche marketing' and how Volkswagen might try to market a product like the Eos. **4**

(c) Quality is important to German car manufacturers like Volkswagen.

(i) Explain the term 'flow production' as used in car manufacturing. **2**

(ii) Discuss the importance of quality management to an organisation such as Volkswagen. **5**

(d) (i) Discuss the importance of liquidity and cashflow management to large organisations. **5**

(ii) Identify and describe the use and benefits of calculating liquidity ratios. **4**

(25)

30 *(a)* A large supermarket announced profits in excess of £2 billion. Sales had increased by 12.4 per cent.

Compare the interests of the following stakeholders in the organisation's financial statements: **4**

- customers
- shareholders.

(b) The increase in sales has largely been achieved by selling music/DVDs, clothing and electrical goods, both instore and online.

(i) Explain the means by which specialist retailers of these products can retain customers. **4**

(ii) Describe the benefits of online selling for the consumer. **4**

(c) Growth for the supermarket requires the employment of new staff.

(i) Describe the selection process which should be used to ensure that the correct person is chosen. **5**

(ii) Once appointed, staff are given induction training. Explain what is meant by this term and the advantages it provides for the new employee. **4**

(d) Discuss the benefits of using ratios to support the figures produced in financial statements. **4**

(25)

Marks

31 *(a)* (i) Explain the following accounting terms: **6**

- gross profit
- cashflow statement
- budget.

(ii) Describe the consequences to an organisation of poor cashflow management. **4**

(iii) Identify and justify two different sources of finance which may be used by an organisation under each of the following headings: **6**

- short-term
- long-term.

(b) Describe the impact on organisational structure and organisational culture following a takeover. **4**

(c) (i) Distinguish between national, international and multinational organisations. **3**

(ii) Explain why a multinational organisation may hold a competitive advantage. **2**

(25)

32 Businesses and consumers are worried that petrol prices are continuing to rise.

(a) Describe the external factors that will affect petrol prices. **6**

(b) Petrol firms may attract bad publicity over the high prices. Explain the role of the public relations department within an organisation. **5**

(c) Car manufacturers are spending billions of pounds in developing alternatives to petrol and diesel engines. Explain why it is important for firms to spend large amounts of money on research and development. **6**

(d) Oil companies use 'outsourcing'. Discuss the advantages and disadvantages of outsourcing for an organisation. **8**

(25)

33 *(a)* (i) Describe the main elements in the final accounts of public limited companies. **6**

(ii) Identify three stakeholders of a public limited company and describe how they can influence the organisation. **6**

(b) (i) Describe two objectives for a public limited company and compare them to the objectives of a charity. **4**

(ii) Discuss the advantages and disadvantages of two long-term sources of finance for a charity. **4**

(c) Explain the role of management in a charity. **5**

(25)

Marks

34 Businesses operate in a competitive environment and must respond to external pressures.

(a) (i) Explain how businesses might react to the following changes: **5**

- demand
- competition
- changes in technology
- structure of the labour market.

(ii) A business may expand using horizontal or vertical integration. Explain these terms and the advantages and disadvantages of each type of growth. **5**

(iii) Explain why a business may opt for demerger. **3**

(b) (i) Explain the consequences to an organisation of poor budgetary control. **5**

(ii) Identify and describe the purpose of two ratios that a business may use to assess profitability. **4**

(c) Explain the reasons why a business may decide to group its activities by place/territory. **3**

(25)

Marks

35 *(a)* Public limited companies have a responsibility towards their shareholders, such as to deliver a reasonable dividend each year.

Describe what the following stakeholders expect in return for their interest in a public limited company: **6**

- lenders
- employees
- customers.

(b) On finding that sales are declining, the plc may wish to carry out market research to find out why.

Describe two effective methods of market research which could be used to discover the cause of the problem. **4**

(c) Once the information is obtained, it may be analysed by means of a SWOT analysis before deciding how to improve the situation.

Describe the advantages and disadvantages of using structured decision-making models. **5**

(d) (i) Discuss the suitability of the following marketing tactics when used to address the problem of falling sales: **6**

- discounting prices for a short period of time
- loss leaders
- buy one get one free.

(ii) Low sales may result in poor cashflow. Identify four other causes of poor cashflow. **4**

(25)

36 The armed forces tend to use a hierarchical structure in their organisation, whereas many firms now prefer to use a flat structure.

(a) (i) Discuss the advantages and disadvantages of switching from a tall to a flat structure. **6**

(ii) Describe why some organisations may decide to use a matrix structure. **3**

(b) (i) Describe methods that an organisation may use to increase staff motivation. **4**

(ii) Describe the actions which an organisation should take when there is disagreement between management and employees. **3**

(c) The use of different payment systems may help to motivate staff. Identify and describe three payment systems which a manufacturer could use. **6**

(d) Explain why many staff stay loyal to the organisation. **3**

(25)

EXAM STYLE QUESTIONS

Marks

37 Supermarkets and restaurants have been forced to remove products due to evidence that they received products from manufacturers which the EU and UK Government consider illegal.

(a) Describe three other means by which legislation can affect the following functional areas of a supermarket: **6**

- marketing
- operations.

(b) The Health and Safety at Work Act also affects the human resource function. Explain the duties of the: **4**

- employer
- employee

in ensuring that this Act is implemented correctly.

(c) Discuss the costs and benefits to retailers and consumers of using a retailer to distribute food products. **7**

(d) (i) A food scare was highlighted on national television and in the newspapers. Explain the reliability of the media in informing the public of such an important issue. **4**

(ii) Describe and justify two means of promotion which could be used by organisations to restore consumer confidence in products which have received bad publicity. **4**

(25)

38 Pepsi have re-established themselves as the number one soft drink ahead of rival Coca-Cola, through the use of clever marketing techniques.

(a) (i) Describe some of the marketing strategies that a company such as Pepsi may use to re-establish its dominant position in the market place. **5**

(ii) Explain the benefits to a company of developing products for a niche market. **3**

(b) Explain the reasons for allocating a large budget to research and development. **3**

(c) (i) Explain and justify the use of a budget to control expenditure. **4**

(ii) Outline the options which may be available to a company facing a short-term cash crisis. **3**

(iii) Explain the purpose of calculating ratios. **3**

(d) Distinguish between a centralised and a decentralised structure. **4**

(25)

				Marks
39	*(a)*	(i)	Explain how works councils can improve employee relations in the workplace.	**4**
		(ii)	Describe two other methods of ensuring good employee relations.	**4**
	(b)		Good employee relations could be described as a strategic objective. Corporate social responsibility is another.	
		(i)	Discuss the tactical decisions that should be made in order to achieve corporate social responsibility.	**5**
		(ii)	Describe the factors that might affect the quality of a decision.	**4**
	(c)		Many successful organisations have become 'customer focused'. Using a customer grouping could help to achieve this goal.	
		(i)	Discuss the advantages and disadvantages of using this type of grouping.	**4**
		(ii)	Identify and describe two other types of grouping.	**4**
				(25)
40	*(a)*	(i)	Explain the differences between a job description and a person specification.	**4**
		(ii)	Explain the importance of providing induction training for new staff.	**3**
		(iii)	Discuss the options available to an employer where relations with employees have broken down, resulting in strike action.	**5**
	(b)	(i)	Describe the changes in an organisation which moves from a hierarchical structure to a flat structure.	**4**
		(ii)	Discuss the effects of de-layering on an organisation.	**4**
	(c)	(i)	Explain the term 'takeover'.	**2**
		(ii)	Describe three sources of finance that could be used to expand a business.	**3**
				(25)

EXAM STYLE QUESTIONS

Marks

41 A newspaper item recently accused a charity of mismanaging the funds it had raised for its cause.

(*a*) Explain the action which a charity could take to improve its public image, having been the victim of a bad press report. **3**

(*b*) (i) Discuss the reliability of written information. **5**

(ii) Choose three different types of information and explain how each can be used effectively by a charity. **6**

(*c*) Describe the contents of the accounting statements in which stakeholders would be able to monitor the financial performance of organisations such as charities and plcs. **6**

(*d*) Explain how the objectives of a charity and a partnership might differ. **5**

(25)

42 A recent strike by British Airways staff has been reported as costing the firm millions of pounds.

(*a*) Describe other forms of industrial action that employees could take, and explain how they would affect the organisation. **6**

(*b*) Describe the role of the human resources department within the organisation. **4**

(*c*) Explain how legislation will affect the running of a business in the areas of: **9**

- health and safety
- employment
- use of ICT.

(*d*) In the 1990s British Airways had to 'downsize' in order to remain profitable. Describe the meaning of this term, and explain how it will affect the organisation. **6**

(25)

				Marks
43	*(a)*	(i)	Describe reasons why an organisation may decide to invest in new ICT equipment.	**4**
		(ii)	Identify and explain two pieces of legislation which may impact on an organisation's use of ICT.	**6**
	(b)	(i)	Explain the term 'mission statement'.	**2**
		(ii)	Explain why it is important for an organisation to have a mission statement.	**3**
	(c)	(i)	Explain the reasons why an employer may carry out staff appraisal.	**3**
		(ii)	Describe the benefits to employees of having a system of staff appraisal.	**3**
		(iii)	Discuss the consequences for an employee whose staff appraisal results in an unsatisfactory report.	**4**
				(25)

44 Staff training and development is essential for regular updating of skills and to maintain motivation.

(a)	(i)	Explain the terms 'on-the-job' training and 'off-the-job' training.	**4**
	(ii)	Describe the costs and benefits to an organisation of undertaking a programme of training and development.	**5**
	(iii)	Explain why staff appraisal is important to both employers and employees.	**4**
(b)		Managers in an organisation are responsible for making decisions. Explain the difference between strategic, tactical and operational decisions, and give an example of each type of decision.	**6**
(c)	(i)	Explain why good marketing is essential to the success of a new product.	**3**
	(ii)	Describe three different types of marketing activity that an organisation may use to market a new product or service.	**3**
			(25)

EXAM STYLE QUESTIONS

Marks

45 *(a)* Businesses operate in a competitive environment.

Describe how the following elements of the marketing mix can be used to increase market share. **7**

- pricing strategies
- promotional activities.

(b) A well-trained workforce contributes towards business success. Compare the advantages and disadvantages of training for an organisation. **6**

(c) In order to remain competitive, businesses have to react to change. Explain how a business might have been influenced by the following changes: **4**

- increase in the number of women in full-time employment, who have children of pre-school age
- increased amount of leisure time
- increased awareness of health issues
- a new competitor entering the market.

(d) Gathering information by use of questionnaire is one method which a business might use to obtain information about their market.

(i) Describe the advantages of using a written postal survey. **5**

(ii) Explain the advantages of using quota sampling when issuing questionnaires. **3**

(25)

Solutions – Case Study Questions

Marks

Case Study 1 Burns Express

1 • Human resources — **10**
   - staff training required – expensive
   - sourcing and employing new staff
- Operations
   - delivery of certain types of parcels proved to be expensive
   - costs of new IT infrastructure
   - purchase of new vehicles
- Marketing
   - lots of competition from other firms in the same sector
   - must establish themselves in a new market
   - large costs of advertising
   - costs of diversification
- External
   - changes to government legislation has had an impact

2 *(a)* Internal finance is cost-free and readily available, but it may limited. External finance will have to be repaid with interest, but more money may be able to be borrowed than is available from internal sources. — **4**

(b)
- Grant – may be available from local or central government. — **2**
- Banks – offer advice on finance and drawing up business plans.
- Inland Revenue – tax advice.

3 *(a)* Costs: — **4**
- Expensive to maintain and continually upgrade
- Requires staff training and new skills
- Can cause de-motivation of staff

Benefits:
- Increased productivity
- Labour saving
- Saves money
- Leads to improved working conditions

(b)
- Computer programs may be used to help in the decision-making process. — **5**
- Computers can gather and process vast amounts of data to aid decision-making.
- ICT may provide the most cost-effective decisions.

SOLUTIONS

Marks

4 • Promotions **3**
- Advertising – television, newspapers, magazines, radio, outdoor media
- Product endorsement

5 *(a)* • It develops a quality image for the business. **5**
- Customers benefit from quality products.
- Business may be able to charge a premium for premium products.
- Repeat business is more likely.
- New product development will be influenced by previous working practice.

(b) • Road – extensive road network in UK and relatively inexpensive. **6**
- Rail – fast, but rail network does not cover all of the country.
- Air – expensive, and road transport is often then required from the airport to final destination.
- Sea – slow method of transport and usually dependent on road transport from port to final destination.

6 • Flat **4**
- Centralised
- Matrix

7 On-the-job training: training is carried out at the employee's normal place of work and during work time. **3**

Off-the-job training: training is carried out at a different location from the normal place of work.

8 • Political factors **4**
- Economics factors
- Social factors
- Environmental factors
- Technological factors

Descriptions/examples should be included.

(50)

Marks

Case Study 2 Soft Fruits

1 • Marketing **10**
  - Competition from other growers
  - General fall in demand for fresh fruit last year
  - Canned fruit, jam and jelly no longer popular
- Operations
  - Scottish crop late to ripen
  - Lack of supplies forcing price up
  - Supply chain needs to be as short as possible
  - Mechanised picking not very successful
  - Fruit can be spoiled by weather and birds
  - Plants produce fruit for only a short time in the season
- Human Resources
  - Seasonal work not attractive to adult workforce
  - Monotonous task
  - Student employees have difficulties with English language

2 *(a)* • High price can be set to give image of quality. **3**
- Advertising in expensive, glossy magazines.
- Product can be made available only in exclusive outlets.
- Product placement where the firm pays for its products to be used in films, for example.

(b) • Testing product at several points in the production process. **6**
- Discard any faulty produce.
- Make sure raw materials are of suitable quality.
- Make sure labour force is trained.
- Make sure machinery is working effectively.
- Use TQM process.

3 • Time **4**
- Cost
- Nature of the product (e.g. weight, perishable product)
- Destination and availability of transport method
- Whether or not the organisation outsources transportation

4 • Enables organisation to gain competitive edge **4**
- Enables organisation to improve existing products
- May find a more efficient process
- Helps the organisation provide for the future needs of customers

5 • Change packaging **4**
- Change price
- Change promotion
- Change name
- Change channel of distribution

SOLUTIONS

Marks

6 • Piece rate **4**
  - Workers are paid per item of output.
  - The faster they work, the more they are paid, therefore quality may suffer.
- Hourly rate
  - Workers are paid the same regardless of quantity produced.
  - Workers can take their time and concentrate on producing quality.

7 *(a)* • Bank loan – money borrowed from bank and paid back in instalments with interest. **4**
- Debentures – a form of loan carrying interest which is usually repaid.
- Share issue – shares are sold in the company, giving shareholders control.

(b) • Capital employed ratio could be considered. **2**
- Check to see if productivity has increased.
- Check to see if wage bill has been reduced.

8 • Health and Safety at Work Act **4**
- Offices Shops and Railway Premises Act
- Discrimination Acts (affecting Human Resources)

9 • Interactive DVD/CD **5**
- Powerpoint to deliver presentation
- Online training
- Tutor can be contacted by email
- Internet used for research
- Database holding staff records can be searched to identify those needing training.

(50)

Marks

Case Study 3 Robert Wiseman Dairies

1 • Marketing **10**
  - Supermarkets are driving down prices
  - Demand in the market is stagnant/the market is settling down
  - Bad publicity from probe on price-fixing
- Operations
  - Difficulties faced with integration from 54 takeovers
  - Speed of growth
  - Currently 20 per cent over capacity
- Finance
  - Heavy investment in new production: risk of failure
  - Farmers want bigger slice of profits
  - Reform of CAP may mean removal of subsidies
- Other
  - Milk business very politicised
  - Not much room for further acquisitions

2 (*a*) • Internal/organic growth – where the business grows naturally as demand and production increase. Can be funded by retained profits, borrowing, selling shares, etc. **6**
- Integration – where the business merges with another in the same industry. Can be at the same stage in the production process – (horizontal), or at a different stage (vertical).
- Conglomerate – where the business takes over or merges with another operating in a different market. This helps to spread the risk for the business.

(*b*) • Political factors such as the Monopolies and Mergers Commission. **4**
- Economic factors such as a recession, when it may be expensive or difficult to raise funds.
- Socio-cultural factors such as the growing unease about globalisation.
- Environmental factors such as protests about the development of green belt sites.
- Competitive factors such as a price war, diverting funds away from growth to market share protection.

3 (*a*) • Selling shares on the stock market can raise large amounts of money for the owners to keep or use to fund development of the business. **5**
- The owners can retain overall control of the business.
- They will have limited liability.
- Part of the business is now owned by other investors.
- The business will now be linked financially to the stock market which could affect confidence in the business.
- The business's accounts will have to be published.

(*b*) • bank loan will normally be for a large amount of money, paid back in instalments over a number of years. **4**
- A mortgage is similar but will be for property – usually a larger amount and repaid over a longer term.
- Debentures are loan certificates sold on the stock market. The lender receives a fixed rate of interest each year. The certificates are for a fixed term and at the end the capital is repaid.

Marks

4 • The nature of the product – for example, products with a short shelf life will have to be delivered quickly, using specialist storage. **5**

- The nature of the market – if the market is widespread it may be necessary to set up regional distribution centres.
- Legal requirements – e.g. there is legislation in place that dictates how livestock are transported.
- The consumers – where consumers would not accept any delays in delivery, plans must be in place to take account of adverse weather or road conditions.
- The business – whether the business wants to control its own distribution and delivery or outsource to a specialist company.

5 *(a)* • They can provide a high degree of personal service. **4**

- Customer loyalty can be built up.
- Responsive to the customers needs.
- Higher staff costs.
- Can be more difficult to control.
- Duplication of some functional areas will be necessary.

(b) • With a functional grouping, the business forms into departments around the main functional areas such as marketing, human resources, etc. **4**

- With a product/service grouping, the business organises around the different products that it produces, setting up divisions for each product grouping.
- With a place/territory grouping, the organisation organises itself around the different areas that it operates in, to better meet the needs of local cultures or tastes.

6 *(a)* • Piecework is where the employees are paid for each good unit that they produce. **4**

- This will encourage the workers to produce as much as possible.
- However, if they are off ill, they may not get paid or are paid only a small amount.
- Bonus is where employees are paid an additional payment when they achieve set targets for sales or production.
- This will encourage them to work to the targets.
- They will get paid their normal wage if they fail to meet the target.
- Performance related pay– where employees can get additional payments for doing their job well.
- Similar to bonus payments.

(b) • Offering non-financial rewards for achieving targets such as certificates. **4**

- Using appraisal schemes to acknowledge good work.
- Offering training schemes to allow for staff development.
- Clear promotion routes for employees.

(50)

Marks

Case Study 4 Aberdeen Airport

1 • Operations **10**
  - Short runways mean large planes cannot land
  - Planes cannot take off with sufficient fuel to travel long distances
  - Lengthier queues due to security
  - Design of buses makes travelling to the airport difficult when passengers have luggage
  - Taxi fare expensive compared with bus fare
  - Train does not provide a direct link to the airport
  - Planes not allowed to land after 10 pm
  - Local residents complain about excessive noise
  - Delayed flights would cause passengers to be bussed from Glasgow or Edinburgh
  - Congestion
  - Lack of trolleys

• Marketing
  - Holidays become more expensive for the consumer when they have to link to another airport
  - Limited choice for Aberdeen consumer
  - Lack of bookings (winter flights to Oslo)
  - Bad press from breach of security
  - Customer satisfaction could be improved

• Finance
  - Cost of new technology to improve security
  - Cost of refurbishing airport
  - Cost of proposed direct link

2 *(a)* Consumers **8**
  - Added convenience of shopping at home.
  - No parking charges.
  - Deliveries are made to the consumer's home.
  - Some goods are unique to the internet.
  - May be a way of obtaining goods from abroad.
  - The consumer knows immediately if the goods are in stock (they may make a wasted journey to the shops).
  - Sound clips can be listened to when purchasing music.

(b) Organisations
  - Organisations can reach a much wider market.
  - They do not have to run a shop which can be costly.
  - Can keep in touch with interested customers by email.

3 • Share issue – where shares are issued for sale to the public through a stock broker or by placing an advertisement in the newspaper. Very large sums of money can be raised in this way, but control of the company may be lost. Dividends also have to be paid. **6**

• Debentures – a group of loans from individuals or other companies. Debenture holders receive annual interest and the loan is eventually paid back. No control is lost.

• Bank loan/mortgage – where money is borrowed from a financial institution and interest paid. Repayment made in instalments so budgeting is easier.

• Venture Capital – venture capitalists will provide finance when banks decide that a loan is too risky. Associated fees are high and the venture capitalists often want part-ownership.

Marks

4
- Customer finds product easily recognisable **4**
- Commands higher selling price
- Can be used to promote goods
- Customer may associate quality with brand name
- Can launch newer products on the back of existing ones
- Brand name may prove to be a valuable assets
- Customers may become loyal to the brand

5 *(a)*
- Shareholders vote at the AGM on proposals. They vote to appoint the Board of Directors and approve the dividend payments. **6**
- Employees can influence by the standard of their work and industrial relations.
- Lenders influence by making finance available to organisations or not. Also they may vary the amount of interest charged.

(b)
- Shareholders would wish to see if the organisation they have invested in is a profitable one. They will compare the returns on their investment with the return they could get elsewhere. **3**
- Employees are interested in the profitability of the firm to see if they are entitled to wage increases, and that their job is secure.
- Lenders are interested in the profitability of the organisation to see if their loans will be returned and the interest paid.

6 *(a)*
- Postal survey, which involves a questionnaire being sent through the post. This is a cheap method to use as it does not need a trained interviewer. **6**
- Telephone survey, which involves a market researcher telephoning people at home and asking them questions. This is a cheap method, and an immediate response is achieved.
- Group discussion, where a group of people are brought together in order to have a discussion. Opinions, feelings and attitudes about the issue being discussed are gained.
- Hall test, where consumers are invited to try out or sample a product and then give their opinions. Opinions, feelings and attitudes are gained (qualitative information).
- Observation, where a person watches consumer activity and records the information. Useful when gathering information on how many cars pass a school entrance at a certain time of day (quantitative information), for example.
- EPOS records customers' shopping habits when they make a purchase at a till. Can provide accurate consumer profiles.

(b)
- The sample of people asked may have been inappropriate, e.g. asking teenagers their opinion on holidays designed for a more mature market. **4**
- The opinions of those asked may have changed by the time the product is launched.
- The questions asked may not have been appropriate to gather the information that the organisation needed to know.
- The people asked may not have been honest in their answers.
- The interviewer may have been biased and led the respondents to give the answer they wished to hear.

7 Quality assurance ensures that quality takes place at all stages in the production process. The aim is to prevent problems happening rather than finding them. Customers' views are taken into account before a product is made or a service provided. Therefore the goods and services will meet the needs of the customer. **3**

(50)

Marks

Case Study 5 Cashmere

1 • Human resources **10**
  - Loss of jobs in textile industry
  - Difficulty in recruiting staff
  - Younger people no longer keen to join industry
- Operations
  - Hand-combed wool makes it a labour-intensive process, which is slow
  - A labour-intensive process is also an expensive one
- Marketing
  - Fashionable item therefore subject to fluctuations in demand
  - Cheaper products available
  - Easier to wash fabrics are in greater demand
  - Department stores looking for cheaper price
  - Bad media coverage
- External
  - Tariffs/trade restrictions
  - Lower wage rates abroad

2 *(a)* Costs: **5**
- Interest will have to be paid on loans/debentures.
- Share issue can be an expensive process.
- Issuing shares or involving venture capitalists may mean losing control.
- Venture capitalists charge high fees.
- Dividends have to be paid to shareholders (long term).

Benefits:
- Grants do not have to be paid back.
- Large sums of money may be obtained which can allow the venture to take place.
- Hire purchase/leasing/trade credit eases cashflow.

(b) • Local enterprise agencies are government-funded organisations which offer advice, training and contacts. **3**
- Trade assocations may provide specialist advice in a particular business or trade area.
- The Inland Revenue offers advice on taxation matters.
- Lawyers offer advice on legal matters.

3 *(a)* Costs: **5**
- Financial costs of courses, travel and accommodation.
- Work time is lost when staff are being trained.
- Output is lost when staff are being trained.

Benefits:
- Increased competency of staff
- Increased flexibility of staff
- Increased motivation of staff
- Increased productivity of staff
- Change easier to introduce
- Improves the image of the organisation

Marks

(b)
- A job description may be drawn up from a job analysis. **5**
- It states the job title, location, tasks, duties and responsibilities.
- Conditions of post may be described, e.g. holiday entitlement, benefits and hours of work.

4
- Inflation is a measure of the increase in prices – this can affect costs of raw materials and wages, which may have to be passed on in the price of the final product. **4**
- Exchange rate – the amount of one currency which can be purchased with another. This varies according to demand and supply of the currency. If the value of sterling is high in comparison to other currencies, UK firms find selling products abroad difficult, as they appear more expensive.
- Interest rates – the interest paid on money borrowed. If the interest rate is high then borrowing for expansion or new product development becomes expensive and affects the cashflow of the business.
- Recession – a period in an economic cycle when unemployment rises. Consumers have less money to spend and this results in lower sales for many businesses. Sellers of luxury products will suffer first.

5 (a)
- Symbol acts as a marketing tool. **4**
- Product may command a higher price.
- Sets a standard which manufacturer must adhere to.
- Brand loyalty may result.
- Consumers perceive the product to be one of quality.
- May be a guarantee that the product has been tested.
- If displayed on the product, it may show the consumer to have an upmarket image.
- Guaranteed that the product is genuine and not a fake.

(b)
- Consumers respond to brand images which celebrities project. **2**
- Consumers can aspire to have the same image as the celebrity.
- Celebrities are photographed/seen on television wearing branded product, and this is a form of promotion.
- Celebrities may appear in advertisements, which draw more attention
- Promotional activities involving celebrities draw more attention.
- Due to enhanced image of product, it may command a higher price.

6 (a)
- Written information can be referred to again; e.g. a newspaper advertisement can be looked at more than once. **6**
- Written information is useful when it is important that information is remembered, such as a phone number to call the seller to purchase the product.
- Lots of written information (direct mail) may be ignored and it is expensive to distribute.
- Moving images cannot be used in the advertisement.

(b)
- Oral information can be easily forgotten.
- Oral information allows opinions to be given and questions to be asked.
- Oral information is easily absorbed when advertising, e.g. television advertising.

				Marks
7	*(a)*	•	This is a method of improving quality.	**3**
		•	The best techniques used by another organisation are employed.	
		•	Used to set standards within an organisation who will then strive to be the best producer.	
	(b)	•	Allows company to find out the needs of its market and then meet them.	**3**
		•	Different products can be produced for different segments.	
		•	Money is not wasted on targeting the wrong segment.	
				(50)

Marks

Case Study 6 Shipbuilding

1 • External 10
- Competition from abroad – Poland and the Far East
- European competition regulations
- Political interference

• Operations
- More work needed for the long term.
- Business 'ups and downs' – difficult to plan for
- Better planning needed for the industry
- History of delays in completions

• Human Resources
- Skills shortage
- Threat to workforce jobs at Ferguson
- Workers will become de-motivated with uncertainty over the future of Ferguson

• Finance
- Large amount of money invested in BAE, may not see a return
- Subsidies are paid to foreign yards
- Ferguson does not seem to attract government assistance.

2 *(a)* • Ships are built to the customers' exact specification. 4
- Orders tend to come in one a time.
- Ships can take many months or even years to complete.
- They require a lot of different skilled workers to build.
- The cost of the finished product is high.

(b) Batch production: 6
- Useful when the business makes a range of similar product, such as in the food industry.
- Allows for flexible production.
- Stocks of partly finished good can be stored and completed later – allows for quick response to new orders.
- Expensive to run small batches of production.
- Time delays and costs in setting up equipment for each run.

Flow production:
- Benefits from economies of scale.
- Easier to build quality systems into the operations process.
- Can use automated production.
- Products often cannot be altered for individual customers.
- Expensive to set up.

3 *(a)* • To regenerate areas of industrial decline. 2
- To provide work in areas of high unemployment.
- To keep production of what could be seen as an essential industry.

(b) • A bank loan can obtain a large amount of money, paid back in instalments over a number of years. 4
- A mortgage is usually a larger amount and is repaid over a longer term.
- Debentures – loan certificates sold on the stock market. Can raise a large amount of money, and fixed outgoings make it easier to plan.

Marks

4 *(a)*
- Suppliers can increase or decrease prices, credit terms or delivery times. **6**
- The effectiveness of managers' decisions will affect how well the organisation achieves its objectives.
- Customers can decide whether or not to buy the products.
- Shareholders can vote at the AGM or add to or withdraw their investment.
- Banks/lenders can refuse finance or alter interest rates.
- Local community can protest or make complaints to local council.

(b)
- Legislation may restrict the organisation's activities. **5**
- Changes in exchange rates may affect the organisation's ability to trade internationally.
- Changes in consumer trends may affect the demand for the organisation's products.
- New technology may not be effective in helping the organisation achieve its goals.
- Other businesses in the market may reduce the demand for the organisation's products.

5 *(a)*
- Budgets are financial plans for the coming months/years. **5**
- Managers have to remain within budget.
- Ensures that any excess spending is highlighted early.
- Allows for delegation without loss of control.
- Will allow for effective monitoring and control of the organisation.

(b)
- Profitability ratios will highlight problems with selling prices, expenses, and cost of supplies. **5**
- Ratios highlight trends within the business.
- Liquidity ratios show how well the business is able to meet its short-term debts.
- Efficiency ratios show how well the business uses its assets.
- Where problems are identified, action can be taken.

(c)
- The trading account shows the profit on buying and selling goods. **3**
- The profit and loss account shows how much profit the business has made from all its activities.
- The net profit will be used to calculate how much tax the business will pay.
- The balance sheet shows what the business is worth, where the money came from and how it was used.

(50)

Marks

Case Study 7 Baxters Foods

1 • Marketing **10**
  - Change in approach could involve financial investment
  - May not be successful
- Operations
  - Need to continually invest and upgrade production methods and equipment
  - Some methods employed were revolutionary and therefore a substantial risk
- Corporate management
  - Risk that the business may not grow or develop properly with family members always leading and managing
  - Investment and takeover into new areas and countries requires new expertise
  - Introduction of non-executive directors may increase risks
- External
  - Such a successful business may be subject to a takeover from other large organisations
  - The company will face different types of competition in each country that it operates

2 *(a)* A person who successfully develops a business idea, combining the factors of production to produce a product or service. **2**

(b) **4**
- Intelligence
- Good business sense
- Confidence
- Tenacity
- A natural leader

3 *(a)* **8**
- Consideration of concepts such as:
  - pricing strategies
  - branding
  - niche marketing
  - differentiated marketing
  - undifferentiated marketing
  - product life cycle.
- Marketing mix – product, price, place, promotion.

Sufficient explanation of how these concepts combine and contribute to the success of a product is also required. Credit relevant examples.

(b) **4**
- Essential to know its customers and its place in the market.
- Allows planning of new products in response to customer needs and wants.
- May allow for testing of products prior to full introduction to the market.
- Allows competitor analysis and comparison to be carried out.

4 A director who is not an employee of the company and who only gives part of his available time to the company. Usually a person with particular experience or skills who holds a seat on the board to exercise a steadying influence on board decisions. The legal obligations to the company and creditors are the same as those of an executive director. **3**

			Marks
5	*(a)*	• Bank loan • Owner's capital • Leasing • Trade credit	**3**
	(b)	General benefits could include (for any source): • Ability to save retained profits for other projects. • Trade credit is free. • Leasing removes the problems associated with owning and maintaining fixed assets. • Bank loan allows for easy planning, with a fixed amount being repaid over a fixed period of time.	**2**
6	*(a)*	• Horizontal integration – organisations combining which produce the same type of product or service. • Vertical integration – organisations at different stages of the production process in the same industry combining. • Diversification – organisations operating in different markets join together. • Merger – where organisations join together on equal terms.	**8**
	(b)	• To minimise risk • To 'buy into' other established markets • To reduce set-up costs and time in new market areas	**2**
7	*(a)*	The entire system of manufacture and production used by the organisation.	**2**
	(b)	• Establishes the brand. • Consumers associate a particular level of quality with the name. • High quality products can lead to a good reputation. • High quality means that a higher price (premium) can be charged.	**2**
			(50)

SOLUTIONS

Marks

Case Study 8 DC Thomson

1 • Marketing **10**
  - Changing tastes of the consumer
  - Competition from Bob the Builder and Postman Pat
  - Sales have dropped
  - Sales heavily dependent on free gifts (an additional cost)
  - Reluctance to allow characters to be used for merchandising
  - Branding building has been conservative
  - General fall in profits in the newspaper industry
  - Links with McDonald's are short term
  - Competition from television and computer games
  - Boring image
  - Need to update image of character due to political correctness/trend toward a healthier lifestyle
  - Poor quality of paper
  - Older market segment only attracted to newspaper (limited)
  - Advertisers wish to cut costs so reduce the amount of advertising they purchase in papers

• Operations
  - Inconsistent quality of printing
  - Dependence on wholesaler for distribution
  - Supermarkets make it easier for consumers to return comics to shelf

• Finance
  - Development of new products carries financial risk
  - Cost of new technology
  - Cost of training
  - Unsuccessful investments
  - Financial concerns reflected in the fact that salary pension payments were not made

2 • Offering the consumer the first few issues free provided they give the company their debit/credit card details will hopefully mean that consumers will sign up for the free magazines and not cancel the order once the free offer time has expired. This could be used to try the magazine for the first time, but also to encourage subscription as a means of buying regularly. **5**

• Offering the magazine at a discounted price would be successful for both (a) and (b).

• Free gift with magazine is more likely to be successful for (b).

• Subscribers (annual) could be given a discounted price, or special deals on purchases available from the magazine, or free gift if they take out a subscription.

• Television advertising is frequently used to make consumers aware of new magazines.

• Direct mail could be used to encourage consumers to try out a new magazine (b). This would be also be a satisfactory way to send out subscription application forms (a).

Marks

3 (*a*) • Stock details can be held on a database. Additions and issues of stock can take place by entering the details by reading barcodes. **5**

- This allows printouts of stock records to be obtained much more quickly. Searches can be carried out to provide management with information, e.g. best-sellers and non-movers, amount of raw materials available.
- Systems can be programmed to order stock immediately when the reorder level is reached.
- ICT can also be used in designing and manufacturing products and for testing prototypes – computer aided design, robots, computer aided manufacture.

(*b*) • Changing the appearance, product recipe or packaging **2**

- Increasing promotional activity
- Encouraging people to use the product more frequently
- Targeting a different market
- Finding a new market
- Finding a new use for the product

4 (*a*) The return on capital ratio (NP/Capital x 100) shows the percentage return on the investment. This can be compared with alternative investments to see if it is worthwhile. **2**

(*b*) • Comparison has to be made to see if the return is better or worse than previous years. **2**

- Ratios do not take account of developments in the pipeline or excessively good trading conditions for the one year.

(*c*) Internal sources of finance such as retained profits or selling assets involve no payment of interest or loss of control. However, selling assets means that the firm may be left without essential equipment. Internal sources may not raise sufficient cash. Investors may provide large amounts of cash, but shareholders have voting rights and may control or influence the organisation strongly. Dividends will also have to be paid. **4**

5 (*a*) • Managers want the organisation to be successful in order to gain status and responsibility. They too are employees and want to make sure they receive a salary. **4**

- Customers look for the best quality products at a satisfactory price.
- The Government wishes the organisation to succeed as it provides employment, generates wealth within the country and pays taxes.
- Suppliers want to receive repeat orders.
- Local community wish the organisation to provide jobs and hence wealth for the area.

(*b*) • Discuss the matter with the human resources manager. **4**

- Approach a trade union representative who will discuss the matter with management on behalf of all workers.
- Development of negotiation, consultation, arbitration and collective bargaining.
- Role of ACAS.

Marks

6 *(a)* Costs:

- Financial cost of courses, accommodation and travelling
- Work time lost when staff are being trained
- Lost output when staff are being trained

Benefits: **5**

- Increased competency of staff
- Increased flexibility of staff
- Increased staff motivation
- Increased productivity
- Change easier to introduce
- Improved image of organisation if seen as a place to receive good training

(b)

- Find out if productivity has increased. **3**
- Find out if accident rate has reduced.
- Evaluate training by questionnaire or interview.
- Find out if staff motivation has increased (evidence might be attendance or turnover).

7 Costs: **4**

- Unnecessary duplication of resources across the different products.
- Divisions may find themselves competing with each other for resources.

Benefits:

- Each division can be more responsive to changes regarding their particular product.
- Expertise can develop within each division regarding their product.
- Easier to identify which areas are doing well and those which are not.

(50)

SOLUTIONS

Marks

Case Study 9 Tilly Confectionary

1 • Marketing **10**
  - Limited outlets or consumer awareness for their product
  - Problems of operating in a high price niche market
  - Health concerns with eating too much sugar/unhealthy product
  - Competition from mass manufactured products
  - Will not have much say in how their product is sold at Tesco
  - High dependence on the internet
- Operations
  - Quality product requires quality ingredients – may be expensive and supply may not be consistent
  - Limited shelf life means product can easily spoil
  - Fast turnaround needed from order to delivery
  - Reliance on outside delivery firm
- Human resources
  - Need to recruit and train workers
  - Workers in the food industry need to be qualified and certificated
  - Low paid job – shortage of labour
- Other
  - Increase in credit card fraud
  - Fixed delivery charge may dissuade small buyers, and lead to a loss of profits for large orders

2 *(a)* • Trade associations are groups of producers in the same industry who come together to support their industry. **4**
- The Business Start Up scheme offers advice and training to support new businesses.
- The Prince's Trust can offer financial support and advice to young people starting up their own business.
- Banks provide business advisors to help small businesses run efficiently.
- Lawyers and accountants provide advice on the legal aspects of setting up the business, and accountants give advice on running the business.

(b) • The effectiveness of the managers' decisions will influence how well the organisation meets its objectives. **4**
- Managers have to define the objectives of any decision.
- Managers have the responsibility of making sure that all staff understand the decision and why it was made.
- Managers have to monitor and control the implementation and evaluate the decision.

3 *(a)* • Can sell to consumers directly in their home **6**
- Can provide a wider range of products
- No need to open more shops
- Reaches a much wider market

- The organisation has to set up a website and distribution network.
- They have to secure the site and offer fraud protection.
- Competitors have easy access to the information.
- Not all consumers have access to the internet.

Marks

(*b*)
- Databases could be used to hold employee information. **4**
- Employees' bank accounts can be automatically credited with pay.
- Databases could be compiled with consumer information.
- Websites could be set up to sell products online.
- Spreadsheets could be used to prepare production budgets.
- Databases could be set up with supplier details.
- Spreadsheets can be used to record financial transactions.
- Spreadsheets can be used to carry out 'what if' analysis.

4 (*a*)
- Allows the organisation to employ specialists. **6**
- Allows business to concentrate on core activities.
- Business no longer has to staff or accommodate the function.
- Specialist firm may produce at lower cost.
- Will lose control of that part of their business.
- Specialist firm may not meet standards required.
- Communication problems between the firms may arise.
- Confidential information may have to be shared with the specialist company.

(*b*) (i)
- Brand names can be sold at higher prices. **4**
- Consumers can easily identify the product.
- Consumers associate a brand name with quality.
- Consumers become loyal to the brand.
- The brand name may become a valuable intangible asset.

(ii)
- Levels of taxation including VAT affect the demand for premium products. **5**
- Health promotions and advice from the government affect eating habits.
- When the economy is in recession, demand for premium products will fall.
- Changes in tastes and attitudes such as healthier eating affect premium products.
- More efficient production will increase the quality and choice of cheaper alternatives.
- Premium products can be highly profitable and will attract competition.

5 (*a*)
- It will increase the competence of the workforce. **4**
- It improves staff flexibility.
- It will be easier to introduce necessary changes.
- Production levels will increase.
- Efficiency will increase and waste decrease.

(*b*)
- Working time is lost while the employee is being trained. **3**
- This could lead to inefficiencies and/or customer complaints.
- Training can be very expensive for the organisation.
- Employees will find it easier to secure a better job and leave.

(50)

Marks

Case Study 10 Thomson Holidays

1 • Human resources **10**
  - Difficult to exercise control over so many employees spread throughout many different countries

• Operations
  - Company perception among consumers may be blurred due to rebranding
  - High costs of rebranding
  - Control over all divisions could be difficult

• Marketing
  - High cost of marketing new brand
  - Different marketing techniques and strategies required in different countries

• Other
  - Large multinational company could be difficult to control

2 *(a)* Promotional activity – attracts new customers **6**
- To establish the brand and what it stands for
- Penetration pricing
- Price discrimination
- Website/e-commerce
- Advertising using a variety of different media

(b) This involves splitting consumers into different groups, e.g. by age, religion, occupation, income, geographical location. **2**

(c) **3**
- Known to consumers
- Has established values attached
- Represents the image of the company

3 *(a)* **4**
- Less risky than merger
- More cost-effective
- Has the necessary infrastructure and experience to be able to grow in this way
- To maximise income and profits

(b) Horizontal integration occurs where two firms producing the same type of product or providing the same type of service, combine. **5**

Vertical integration occurs where firms at different stages of production in the same industry combine.

Either method of integration may be suitable to an organisation such as Thomson. For example, Thomson may join with another holiday company to form a larger organisation.

4 *(a)* **4**
- Difficulties in communication
- Difficult to manage staff who are based in another country
- Large number of staff to manage – need to be split into teams
- Difficult to have a consistent approach

(b) **3**
- On-the-job training
- Off-the-job training
- Demonstration
- Coaching
- Staff development

Marks

(c) Employment Rights Act 1996 states a wide range of duties and rights of an employer and employee. **4**

Health and Safety at Work Act 1974 states employers' and employees' duties with regard to health and safety in the workplace.

5 Budgets are used to monitor and control expenditure. Businesses such as Thomson are large and deal with huge amounts of money. The use of budgets allows such large organisations to monitor and control their costs, set targets for divisions/departments, plan for future developments and expenditure, and plan for cash shortages. **4**

6 (a) Organisational culture refers to the beliefs, values and norms that are shared by all the staff working for the organisation. **2**

(b) **3**

- Planning
- Commanding – taking charge of situations
- Co-ordinating activities
- Controlling – taking responsibility
- Organising

(50)

Marks

Case Study 11 Scottish Whisky

1 • Marketing **10**
  - Product is seen as one for the older, male consumer
  - Tastes change quickly
  - Prices may have to be increased to cover losses incurred because of a decline in the value of the dollar
  - Labelling and naming of product may be misleading consumers
  - Large amount of competition
  - Cost-cutting war with competitors
- Operations
  - Difficulty in obtaining stocks for US market
  - Removing European stocks might leave European market short
  - Labels need to be changed, which increases costs
- External
  - Decline in value of dollar makes goods expensive in US, therefore demand may drop
  - Profits may drop if producers absorb the costs
  - Government campaign and media coverage of health crisis
  - Legislation on licensing laws may reduce consumption
  - High tax increases price for consumer

2 *(a)* • Can the supplier be depended on to supply goods as promised? **4**
- Can the supplier provide goods at short notice?
- What are the additional costs?
- How long will the delivery take?
- Is the price satisfactory?

(b) • A cheaper price might be available but the quality of the goods may be lower. **2**
- Delivery delays may cause production to stop.
- Quicker delivery times may be charged for.

(c) • Customers will know that they are buying a quality product/service, and will purchase the organisation's products before those of a competitor. **3**
- A quality symbol may be appreciated by a consumer as it enhances their personal image.
- The manufacturer may command a higher selling price for 'quality'.

3 Flow production is used when the final output is high and the products are identical. This means that costs are spread over a large output, and therefore the cost per unit is reduced. An automated process lowers labour costs. **3**

Batch production is used when an organisation such as a baker makes one batch of products before moving on to the next one. Batches can be changed to meet specific requirements.

Job production is less likely in the food and drink industry, except perhaps for something like a wedding cake. One-off requirements can be met, and specifications changed even if production has started.

			Marks
4	*(a)*	Young people consider branding to be important as it enhances their personal image; therefore trainers and clothing have to be identifiable. This allows the person to feel part of the youth culture. People from higher income grouping may consider the purchase of branded products to be important as it allows them to show that they have a high income. Cheaper products are considered inferior and something they do not buy – this is snob value.	**2**
	(b)	• Discount their prices to undercut the own label brand. • Maintain a high price to make the customer think that the branded product is of a higher quality. • Promotions such as buy one, get one free, or advertising. • Celebritity endorsement. • Pay for premium shelf position within the retail outlet.	**4**
5	*(a)*	• To remove a competitor • To increase market share • To increase profits • To diversify • To obtain the assets/brand name of a competitor • To invest cash reserves	**4**
	(b)	• Consumers may not be affected by a takeover at all, as the business taken over will run as before – only ownership changes. • Consumers may find that the business they have been using vanishes and the products are replaced by those of the firm taking over, e.g. Morrisons' takeover of Safeway. • Reduced choice for the consumer in the market. • Reduced number of competitors may mean an increase in price. • An offer may be made to shareholders to purchase their shares. If they agree they receive cash, but lose their shareholding and therefore control. • If the business makes more profits as a result of a takeover (economies of scale) then the shareholder receives more dividend. • Employees may lose their jobs as a result of the takeover if it is decided to streamline the business and remove all duplication of resources. • Employees may find a change in their working conditions because of having a new employer.	**6**
6	*(a)*	• Discounts available for bulk purchasing • Delivery time of suppliers • Quantity required for production or sale • Nature of the product – is it perishable? • Amount of floor space • Cash available to purchase stock	**4**
	(b)	• Balance sheet shows the value of a business at a particular date • Lists the cost price, depreciation and current value of fixed assets • Shows the value of current assets, e.g. stock, debtors, bank and cash • Shows the amount of liabilities held by the firm – creditors, loans, expenses due • Shows the amount of capital – the investment by the owner • Shows the amount of drawings – the amount of profits withdrawn by the owner	**4**

Marks

7 *(a)*
- Retailers display and sell the product. **2**
- Retailers allow the product to be distributed in many more places.
- Manufacturers may receive direct orders from large retailers. This may allow discounts for bulk purchasing, which may be passed on to the consumer.

(b)
- Reaches a far wider market (worldwide). **2**
- Sales can be made 24 hours per day
- Consumer can shop from the convenience of their own home and have the goods delivered.
- In the early stages, an online retailer may have the competitive edge.

(50)

Marks

Case Study 12 Lingo24

1 • Marketing **10**
  - The market for translation services is very competitive
  - They have no strategy for selling off line
  - Low price strategy may be seen as reflecting low quality
- Operations
  - Communication difficulties across countries
  - Ethical policy may slow process down
  - Over reliance on internet/world wide web
  - Quality assurance systems – more difficult to implement over long distance
- Human resources
  - Recruitment in different countries may be problematic, with different employment laws, cultures, etc.
  - Difficult to keep employees motivated when so spread out
  - Some employees may be resistant to ethical policies, particularly in less well-developed nations
- Other
  - Difficulties in financing growth with a lack of traditional assets
  - Some potential clients may not support ethical policy (e.g. airlines)

2 *(a)* • They can provide a high degree of personal service. **4**
- Responsive to the customer's needs.
- Customer loyalty can be built up.

- Duplication of some functional areas will be necessary.
- Higher staff costs.
- Can be more difficult to control.

(b) • With a functional grouping the business forms into departments around the main functional areas such as marketing, human resources, etc. **6**
- The resources of the organisation will be better used.
- Staff will become experts in their own field.
- Staff may put loyalty to the department before the organisation.
- Slow response to changes in the business environment.

- In a product/service grouping, the business organises around the different products that it produces, setting up divisions for each product grouping.
- Each division will be a self-contained unit.
- Easier to identify which part is doing well/less well.
- Duplication of resources.
- Difficult to share research and development.

- With a place/territory grouping the organisation organises itself around the different areas that it operates in.
- You can better meet local cultures or tastes.
- Customer loyalty can be developed.
- Administration can be time-consuming.
- More difficult to control the organisation.

Marks

3 *(a)*
- Technology – more employees working from home, reducing the size of departments. **4**
- Product – having a small number of large customers would see the formation of a matrix structure.
- If the business operates in a small local market, an entrepreneurial or flat structure would be most appropriate.
- If it is a large and diverse market, it may form functional groupings in geographical areas.
- The preference or beliefs of senior management will decide on the structure to be adopted.

(b)
- Flat structure. **4**
- They employ mostly specialists who can work unsupervised.
- There will be few managers.
- Each manager will have a wide span of control.
- There will be a heavy workload on the managers.

4 *(a)*
- Job analysis is carried out to see what vacancy exists. **5**
- Looks at the main physical and mental elements of the job, specific skills required and responsibilities.
- Job description drawn up with overall purpose of the job and main tasks.
- Job description can be used as a basis for the job advert, and to help applicants decide if they should apply.
- Person specification is drawn up to identify the individual who would be best suited for the job.
- It would include the desirable physical attributes, skills, qualifications and experience.
- The organisation must decide whether to recruit internally and/or externally.

(b)
- Application forms should be sent out, allowing comparison of responses to the same set of questions. **3**
- The most suitable should then be invited to interview.
- Aptitude or psychometric testing could be used.
- References should be sought from previous employers or educational establishments.

5 *(a)* Job production: **4**
- Products can be built to the customer's exact specification.
- High degree of skill may be required.
- The cost of the finished product is high.

Flow production:
- Benefits from economies of scale.
- Easier to build quality systems into the operations process.
- Can use automated production.
- Products often cannot be altered for individual customers.
- Expensive to set up.

(b)
- The quality of materials will be reflected in the final product for the consumers. **4**
- The quality of the workforce will affect how well the products are made.
- The quality and reliability of machinery will affect the level of wastage and quality of final output.
- High quality will reduce the number of returns and complaints from customers.

SOLUTIONS

Marks

6 • Debentures – loan certificates sold on the stock market. Can raise a large amount of money, and fixed outgoings make it easier to plan. 6

- The sale of some of its assets to a finance company and then leasing them back – this can raise a large amount of money.
- Selling shares on the stock market/becoming a plc can raise large sums of money.

(50)

Marks

Case Study 13 BAA

1 • Operations 10
  - 100 per cent hold baggage screening will increase staffing costs
  - More staff training will be required, costing more money
- Human resources
  - Increased staff costs due to increased security measures
  - Increased staff training costs
  - Large number of staff means it may be difficult to maintain staff morale
- Corporate management
  - Need to develop staff to maintain company image
  - Need to maintain caring environmental image with the public
- External
  - Environmental pressures
  - Increased security concerns affect business negatively
  - Expansion means they will have to overcome the threats and problems of competition

2 *(a)* Ability to be open and transparent in business practices towards shareholders and all people affected by the business. 2

(b) • Affected by planning restrictions 4
- Noise from increased air traffic
- Overall environmental impact
- Subject to complaints and protests from those who object to the environmental impact created by BAA

(c) • Shareholders – can influence decisions at meetings. 6
- Managers – exert influence over day-to-day running.
- Employees – can affect the operation of the business.

3 *(a)* • Bank loan – money borrowed over a fixed period of time and repayable in monthly instalments with interest. 2
- Retained profits – money retained in the business from previous years.

(b) Environmental: 6
- Operations affected by weather and climate change
- New environmental legislation

Political:
- Changes in taxation or legislation

Economic:
- A downturn in the economy would adversely affect air ticket sales

4 • Important to find out what customers think, for decision-making 5
- Business can change practices in light of findings
- Identifies the target market
- Assesses the effectiveness of current marketing
- More closely match the needs of customers, e.g. promotions

5 The number of sub-divisions within the management structure and their responsibilities. 2

SOLUTIONS

Marks

6 *(a)*
- Employment Rights Act 1996 – gives the employee certain rights following their appointment. **4**
- Employment Equality (Religion or belief) Regulations 2003 – prevents discrimination on the basis of religion or belief.

(b)
- New equipment required **5**
- Increased costs
- More staff training
- Changes to working practices
- Risk assessments need to be carried out

(c)
- Increased staff motivation **4**
- Identifies staff development needs
- Sets goals based on organisational targets
- Produces a better qualified workforce
- Attracts high quality staff to the organisation

(50)

Marks

Case Study 14 Dairy farmers

1 • Marketing **10**
- Bad publicity from protests
- Pressure to increase prices
- Prices too low to ensure supply
- Price is becoming a political issue

• Operations
- There may be over-production in the industry
- May have to import milk at higher prices
- Protests are reducing supply
- Disagreements over supply and demand
- Problems with pricing in supply chain
- Increasing reliance on overseas suppliers

• Finance
- Farmers find it difficult to continue with current pricing structure
- Difficult to invest when future is uncertain
- Processors seem to be taking too much money

• Human resources
- Farmers demotivated
- Reduction in the number of dairy farmers
- US attracting dairy farmers

2 *(a)* **3**
- Price will be set to cover production costs and planned profit.
- Price should take account of competition in the market.
- Price will reflect the quality of the product.
- Price can determine the promotion of the product.

(b) (i) **2**
- Differentiated marketing is used when the product is aimed at a particular segment or segments of the market.
- Undifferentiated or mass marketing is used when the product is aimed at the whole market.

(ii) **4**
- Segmentation allows the organisation to focus their marketing activities at those most likely to buy their product.
- It avoids waste in promoting to areas of the market which are not interested in the product.
- Other segments who might be interested in the product may be unaware of it.
- Focusing on only some parts of the market carries more risk.

Marks

3 (*a*) (i)
- Primary information is gathered by the organisation for a particular purpose. **4**
- Secondary information already exists and was collected for another purpose.
- Quantitative information is factual information based on facts or figures.
- Qualitative information is based on opinions, beliefs, etc.

Internal and external also acceptable.

(ii)
- Management must have good quality information in order to make good quality decisions. **6**
- If the information is historical, it may be out of date and not reflect the current situation.
- If the information contains bias, errors can be made in decision-making.
- The decision must be based on complete information to be the correct decision.
- Management needs good quality information to measure the performance of the organisation.
- Management needs good information in order to identify new business opportunities.

(*b*)
- They can see if the objective was achieved. **3**
- They can ask customers if there has been an improvement.
- They could carry out a SWOT analysis before and after.

4 (*a*)
- Strike – employees withdraw their labour, there is no productivity, and the employer loses sales. **4**
- Go slow – employees do their jobs but very slowly; this slows down production rate and sales levels may fall.
- Overtime ban – employees refuse to work overtime hours so some work will not be completed on time. This may affect late delivery which could include penalties.
- Work to rule – employees only work to their contract and this may reduce productivity.

(*b*)
- Enter into negotiations to try and resolve the situation. **4**
- If no agreement can be reached, they may seek arbitration.
- Arbitration is where an independent arbitrator such as ACAS will listen to both sides and offer a solution.
- Arbitration may be binding, where both parties agree beforehand to abide by the arbitrator's decision.

5 (*a*)
- A sole trader makes all their own decisions, keeps all their profits, and is easy to set up. They have no one to share responsibilities with and find it harder to raise capital. **6**
- A partnership allows for shared responsibility and can bring together complementary skills. Profits have to be shared and disagreements between partners can arise.
- A limited company has limited liability and is relatively straightforward to set up. Shares can be sold to raise additional capital. Profits have to be shared, and there are legal costs in setting up the business.

(*b*)
- Enterprise is needed to bring together and organise the factors of production. **4**
- Enterprise will identify opportunities and gaps in the market.
- It will enable calculated risks to take place so that the organisation can prosper.
- New ideas will be brought to the organisation.

(50)

Marks

Case Study 15 McCowans Highland Toffee

1 • Operations **10**
  - Increasing cost of raw materials
- External Factors
  - Trade protection schemes are partly to blame for pushing up cost of raw materials
  - Movement in the exchange rate has pushed up the cost of raw materials
  - Trend towards healthier eating
  - Food Standards Agency to reduce amount of marketing on confectionery
- Finance
  - Sourcing finance is not easy for smaller businesses
  - Borrowing money is risky as it has to be paid back
  - Loans carry interest which is an additional expense to a firm
  - Risk of being sued by a model for the cost of her dental treatment
- Marketing
  - Product not widely available
  - Not possible to deal directly online
  - Search engines do not give McCowans webpage as the first one
  - Media pressure to stop people consuming so many sweets
  - Vast amount of competitors
  - Competitors are able to spend much more on marketing

2 Delayering is the removal of a tier of management (reducing staff levels). A smaller hierarchy is created where each manager has an increased span of control. **7**

- Improves communication
- Makes decision-making quicker and more effective
- Empowerment of staff
- Cuts costs as there are fewer management salaries to pay
- Allows organisation to respond more quickly to market changes

3 • Bank overdraft – where a customer can arrange to take out more money from their bank account than they have in it. Interest is paid on the amount overdrawn. **6**
- Bank loan – where an agreed amount is borrowed from the bank. Interest is paid on the whole amount borrowed.
- Description of: trade credit, factoring, grant, retained profits, leasing, hire purchase, owner's savings, share issue (private).

SOLUTIONS

Marks

4 Wholesalers: **7**

- Saves manufacturers from making small deliveries to retailers
- Saves manufacturer the costs of holding stocks
- Saves manufacturers from being left with stock if demand falls
- May save manufacturer from labelling, pricing, packaging
- Manufacturers have less control over the way the product is marketed

Retailers

- they make the product available to a wider market geographically
- they are easier to access by the consumer
- they are responsible for displaying, pricing and marketing product
- they may provide information
- they may provide after-sales support
- they decide how the product is sold
- they take a cut of profit which makes the product more expensive for the consumer

5 *(a)* **4**

- Spreads the risk of failure from one product
- Possible to market products so that it appears desirable to have more than one from the range, e.g. shampoo and conditioner
- Meets the needs of different market segments
- Allows entry into other markets, and as a result sales and profits may increase

(b) Description of, e.g.: **3**

- Local newspaper/radio advertising
- Fliers
- Reduction in price
- Buy one, get one free

Needs some differentiation between the large scale television deals/sponsorship possible to the large firm.

6 **5**

- To remove a competitor
- To benefit from economies of scale which reduces costs and therefore it is possible to increase profit
- A means of growth
- They already have knowledge of the market
- They have established contacts to whom they can distribute products
- Already have expertise in the field

Marks

7 *(a)* Development of: **5**

- Quality
- Quantity – can they supply the necessary quantity?
- Price
- Lead time
- Time taken to deliver goods
- Reliability – will they remain in business/will the goods be delivered when promised?
- Location – will it involve delivery charge?
- Discounts for bulk buying
- Are credit terms offered?

(b)

- Records are updated quickly when issues and receipts are made. **3**
- Can be programmed to reorder stock when reorder level is reached.
- Barcodes can be scanned which allows details to be entered quickly and accurately.
- Managers can use the information to check stock levels, best-sellers, non-movers, at any time of the day.

(50)

Solutions – Exam Style Questions

SOLUTIONS

				Marks
1	*(a)*		• Risk taking • Inventive • Good leadership skills • Clear vision • Ability to communicate effectively	**4**
	(b)		• Problem • Objectives • Constraints • Gather information • Analyse the information • Devise possible solutions • Select the best solution • Communicate the decision • Implement the decision • Evaluate the effectiveness of the decision	**6**
	(c)	(i)	• Hierarchical • Flat • Entrepreneurial • Matrix • Centralised/decentralised	**2**
		(ii)	Description of two types of organisational structure from those identified in (c) (i). Maximum of two marks for diagram(s).	**5**
	(d)	(i)	Where a company identifies a gap in the market and produces a product to fill that small gap.	**2**
		(ii)	• Provides information on the size and nature of the target market • Preferences of consumers • Effectiveness of selling methods • Customer perceptions • Effectiveness of advertising and promotions • Costs include expense, difficulties in analysing information collected, poor response to surveys • Benefits include collection of large amounts of information, production of accurate customer profiles, ability to tailor future products to meet consumer needs.	**6**
				(25)

Marks

2 *(a)* Price: **8**

- Reduce all prices below competitors
- Reduce prices on most popular products
- Increase prices on certain products to increase perception of quality

Place:

- Sell over the internet with home delivery
- Open more outlets to restrict opportunities for competitors
- Develop partnerships (e.g. Tesco and BP)

Promotion:

- Embark on advertising campaign
- Develop social responsibility (e.g. computers/books for school)
- Use wellknown celebrities to endorse products

Product:

- Expand product range (e.g. Tesco non-food)
- Develop new products to take account of changing attitudes (e.g. Iceland stocks no GM foods)
- Develop quality range (e.g. Sainsbury's 'Taste the difference' range)

(b) (i) Random sampling: **4**

- There is little chance of bias being introduced.
- It is relatively straightforward to draw up a sample.
- It may not be focused on a market segment.
- When someone is chosen for the sample they must be interviewed.

Quota sampling:

- The sample is selected in proportion to groups in the population.
- Interviewers can substitute interviewees if the first person chosen is not available.
- Results can be less representative than random.
- There is more opportunity to introduce bias.

(ii) **4**

- The information will be up to date.
- It is collected for the exact purpose it will be used for.
- It is not available to competitors.
- You can go back and ask follow-up questions.
- More likely to be free from bias.

(c) (i) **4**

- Organisations can obtain information about potential customers.
- They can gather information on what products are most popular in which areas.
- They can include a questionnaire to be completed by customers.
- They can receive feedback through email.
- They can find out what groups of customers buy on the internet.

(ii) **5**

- Organisations should obtain and process data fairly and lawfully.
- They have to register the purpose for which the information is held.
- They must not disclose the information in any way that is different from the stated purposes.
- Only hold information that is adequate, relevant and not excessive.
- Only hold information that is accurate and up to date.
- Must not hold the information longer than is necessary.

(25)

Marks

3 *(a)*
- Product – where activities are grouped according to product or product range. Each division can be responsive to changes in its field. Expertise can develop within each division. Can give more incentive for staff to perform better. Management can identify the parts of the business which are not doing so well. **5**
- Place – where activities are grouped according to geographical area. It allows an organisation to cater for the needs of customers in different geographical locations.

(b)
- Damage to the image of one brand does not affect the other brands. **6**
- Different market segments can be targeted.
- Consumer choice can be offered from the same company.
- Each product can be set up as a profit centre in its own right.
- May be the result of a takeover and the product retains the name of the company taken over, to allow customer loyalty to continue.

(c) (i)
- Loss of control over the activity outsourced **4**
- Confidentiality issues
- Quality of work may not be satisfactory
- Time delays
- Cost

(ii) Flow: **4**
- Large scale production
- Mechanised production therefore lower labour costs
- Bulk discounts available for raw materials purchase
- Costs spread over a large output

Batch:
- Different products can be made in batches, e.g. flavours
- Skilled staff not necessary
- Standardised machinery can be used to reduce costs

(d) (i)
- Need to maintain position – marketing reminds customers that the product exists. **3**
- Always have to compete with new products.

(ii)
- Alter the product – change the recipe, launch a new version **3**
- Change the packaging
- Alter channel of distribution
- Change price
- Change promotion
- Change the use which customers have for the product
- Change the name
- Produce product line extensions

(25)

Marks

4 *(a)* Businesses produce goods and services to meet consumer needs and wants. Consumers then buy the goods or services so that they obtain the things that they want. This creates wealth for the business organisations, their employees and their shareholders. Consumers then have money to spend from their wages and salaries and want other goods and services. This cycle is continuous. **4**

(b) An entrepreneur is a person who develops a business idea and combines the factors of production (land, labour, capital and enterprise) to provide a service or produce a product. Entrepreneurs are also known for taking risks and being innovative in their business practices. **6**

(c)
- To stay ahead of and compete with the competition **5**
- To attract the best staff
- To be more efficient
- To reduce costs and save money
- To increase productivity

(d) (i)
- Greater flexibility **5**
- Reduced staffing costs
- Easy to plan with no long-term commitment to staff
- Staff can be utilised as and when required
- Agency staff are often used, removing the burden from the human resources department and giving fast and easy access to new staff

(ii)
- Access to more suitable applicants **3**
- Entire recruitment process is managed outside the organisation
- Saves time
- Agency may be more experienced than the human resources department within the organisation

(iii)
- Equal Pay Act 1970 **2**
- Sex Discrimination Act 1975
- Disability Discrimination Act 1995

(25)

Marks

5 *(a)* – Lion mark on eggs **6**

– Lion mark on toys
– British wool symbol
– Investors in People
– BS5750/ISO 9002
– ABTA symbol

- Customers are assured that they are receiving a quality product or service.
- The organisation can use the symbol as a marketing tool.
- Contracts may be awarded only to organisations holding BS5750 by Government.
- Fewer complaints or returns.
- Brand loyalty established.
- Standard of service may slip after award has been granted.
- Difficult to compare some standards internationally (such as hotel ratings).
- Expensive to set up the process.

(b) Advantages: **6**

- Senior management make decisions for the business as a whole.
- Resources allocated evenly/fairly throughout the organisation.
- Procedures standardised throughout the organisation.
- More experienced decision-makers.

Disadvantages:

- Branch managers are not empowered and therefore their motivation may not be as high as if they were allowed to make decisions
- Local needs cannot be considered.
- Top management have all the stress and responsibility of decision-making.

(c) (i) **4**

- The net profit ratio measures the profit made after expenses have been paid. By making comparisons with previous years or competitors, decisions may have to be taken to cut expenses, or methods introduced to increase gross profit.
- The rate of stock turnover shows how many times the business is selling its stock. If the figure is too low, decisions would be taken to move the slow selling lines, or to reduce the amount of stock held.

(ii) **5**

- Financial accounting information is historical.
- They do not show external factors which affect the business.
- They do not show the implications of future developments.
- They do not include factors like staff morale or turnover.
- If comparisons are made with competitors, the firm chosen must be of a similar type and size for the comparison to be valuable

(d) **4**

- Bookings can be made over the internet, saving staff taking phone calls.
- Double bookings should be avoided if ICT is used.
- ICT can be used for stock control purposes (restaurant and bar).
- Bills can be charged immediately to the customer.
- Staff records can be stored on a database, which can be used for example to decide when staff require training.
- Menus, letters etc can be produced in a more professional way.
- Financial records can be stored in a spreadsheet which can be used for decision-making purposes ('what if').

(25)

Marks

6 *(a)* (i)
- Core staff are permanent full-time staff that the organisation sees as essential for the future. **3**
- Contractual staff are employed on a contract basis for a number of years, usually on projects. They will be released if no longer required when the contract is completed.
- Casual staff are likely to be low skilled staff who are taken on as temporary workers.

(ii)
- Contractual and casual staff will have little loyalty to the organisation. **5**
- They may leave for permanent jobs while still needed.
- The organisation does not have to pay them when they are not needed.
- They will be less motivated than core staff.
- They can be paid less than core staff.
- The administration costs involved in recruiting contractual and casual staff are high.

(b)
- Employees may be more motivated. **5**
- When working from home, the employees will provide their own accommodation, heat, light etc.
- The employer may not have to provide equipment.
- There will be fewer problems with lateness and absenteeism.
- The employee will not have to spend time and money travelling.
- The employee can work at their own pace.
- They do not have to start at a certain time.

(c)
- It is difficult to carry out risk assessment in the employee's home. **4**
- They cannot ensure that employees are taking breaks etc.
- The employer will have to arrange additional health and safety training.
- If they are working with display screen equipment, the employer will have ensure that they have adjustable seating, appropriate lighting etc.

(d) (i)
- The introduction of broadband makes communication much faster. **4**
- Mobile phones allow the organisation to keep in touch without using the home telephone.
- New video telephone services are available on broadband.
- Instant messaging services allow real-time discussion.
- Encryption services allow confidential information to pass safely between the employee and the workplace.

(ii)
- Staff training will be required. **4**
- Staff must be employed to maintain the systems.
- ICT can be very expensive to purchase, as is the cost of updating.
- There is a cost to customer service if the system crashes.

(25)

SOLUTIONS

Marks

7 *(a)*
- Keep all the profits. **4**
- Make your own decisions.
- No need to publish accounts.
- No one to share responsibilities.
- Very stressful – difficult to take holidays/time off.
- More difficult/expensive to borrow money.

(b)
- Suppliers – can increase or decrease prices, credit terms or delivery times. **6**
- Managers – the effectiveness of their decisions affect how well the organisation achieves its objectives.
- Government – changes in legislation or economic policy may force change in the business.
- Customers – can decide whether or not to buy the products.
- Shareholders – can vote at the AGM or add to or withdraw their investment.
- Banks/lenders – can refuse finance or alter interest rates.
- Local community – can protest or make complaints to local council.

(c) (i)
- The quality of information available **5**
- Whether all relevant information is available
- The experience and qualities of the decision maker
- The ability of the decision maker to use decision-making techniques
- Personal interest of the decision maker
- The ability of the decision maker to take risks

(ii)
- Compare the outcome to the objectives of the decision. **4**
- Research customers' opinions before and after.
- Ask staff to comment on the effectiveness of the changes.
- Find out if sales/efficiency has improved.

(d)
- The price charged by the supplier **6**
- Reliability of supplier for delivery times
- Discounts that are available
- Credit terms offered
- Cost of delivery and insurance
- The quantity that can be supplied at one time
- If the supplier has the product available.

(25)

				Marks
8	*(a)*	(i)	• Traditional organisations tend to have tall structures. • Nature of the organisation – e.g. Army will have a tall structure. • A large organisation is more difficult to control so tall is appropriate. • Nature of the product – flat structure suitable for a product with a small number of customers. • Technology may reduce the need for a layer of personnel.	**5**
		(ii)	• Redundancies may occur. • Less wages to pay. • More work may have to be covered by the remaining staff. • Lower of morale due to uncertainty.	**3**
	(b)	(i)	• Limited liability. • Large amount of finance can be raised. • Easier to borrow money. • Easier to grow and dominate the market.	**4**
		(ii)	• Ownership lies with the shareholders who are entitled to vote. • A shareholder with the majority of shares has the most power. • Board of Directors run the company. • Shareholders can sell shares and the ownership changes.	**4**
	(c)	(i)	• Discounted pricing – where prices are reduced. • Advertising on radio, TV, newspapers. • Invite celebrity footballer to play in a charity match. • Issue vouchers to regular supporters for special matches.	**4**
		(ii)	• Good media coverage improves/maintains the image of a club • Organisation may invite media to follow events which will improve their image • Bad media coverage tarnishes the reputation of the club • One incident involving a member of a club can damage the image of the whole organisation • Media coverage of football is widespread and therefore has a large impact on the club	**5**
				(25)

Marks

9 *(a)* • New products will be introduced before older products become unprofitable. **6**

- The business can spread the risk of failure among a range of products.
- Profit levels will be more stable and easier to manage.
- Profitable products can support the development and launch of new products.
- The organisation can appeal to a number of different market segments.

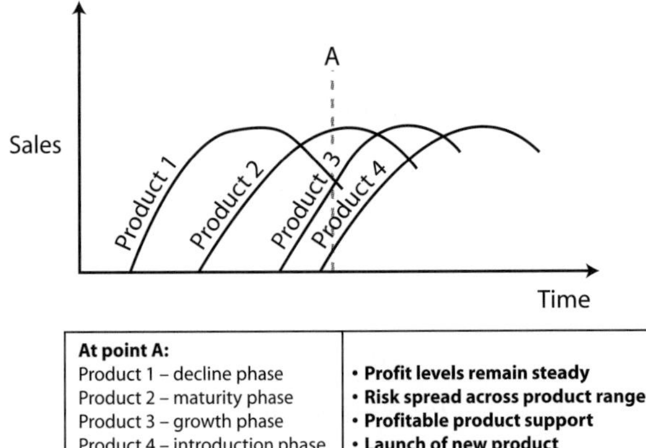

At point A:	
Product 1 – decline phase	• **Profit levels remain steady**
Product 2 – maturity phase	• **Risk spread across product range**
Product 3 – growth phase	• **Profitable product support**
Product 4 – introduction phase	• **Launch of new product**

(b) Overstocking **6**

- This will lead to high costs for storage and maintenance of stock.
- There will be higher insurance costs.
- Additional storage space will be needed.
- Stock may become outdated or deteriorate.

Understocking

- The organisation will be unable to satisfy consumer demand and they may go elsewhere.
- Cost of ordering and transportation will increase as they have to do it more often.
- If there is an increase in demand, they will be unable to cope.
- Stoppages in production may occur as they run out of stock.

(c) • Develop new markets for the product **6**

- Find new uses for the product.
- Promote more frequent use of the product.
- Change the packaging to make it more appealing.
- Add new additional features.
- Carry out promotional activities to renew interest in the product.

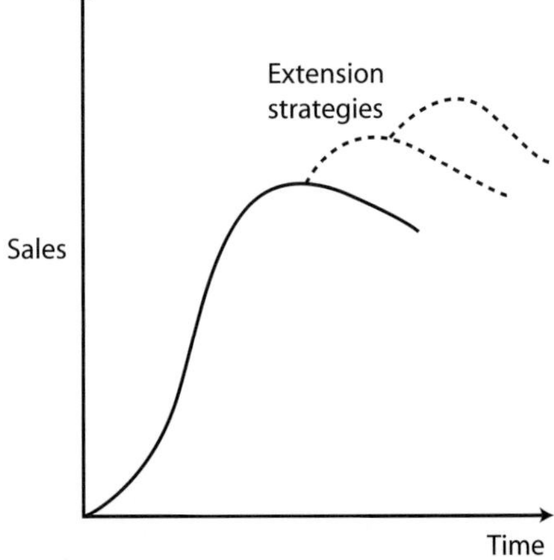

Marks

(d) • SWOT would highlight which products are doing well and which are not. **4**
- It would show which products have potential for the future.
- It would compare products to competitors.
- It may highlight new markets for their products.
- It would show which mix would be the most profitable.

(e) • The effectiveness of the managers' decisions will influence how well the organisation meets its objectives. **3**
- Managers have to define the objectives of any decision.
- Managers have the responsibility of making sure that all staff understand the decision and why it was made.
- Managers have to monitor, control the implementation and evaluate the decision.

(25)

Marks

10 *(a)* Existing products may be nearing the end of the product life cycle and therefore the organisation needs to launch new products on the market for survival: **4**

- To enter new markets
- To increase sales/profits
- To spread the risk
- As a means of growth

(b) **3**

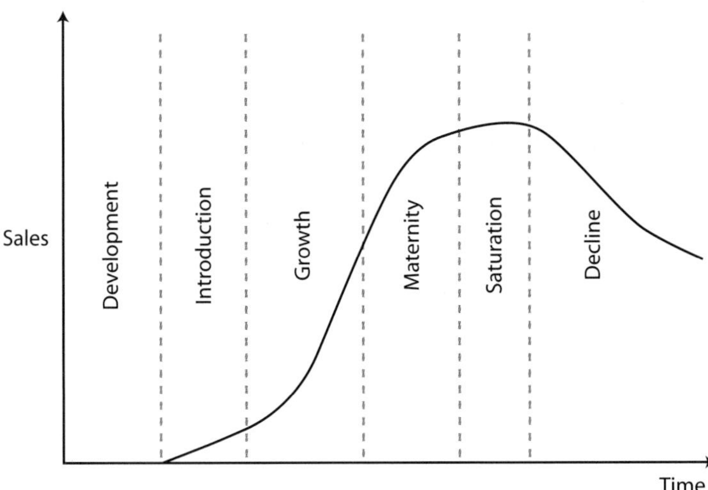

Description of:

- Change packaging
- Improve product
- Alter channel of distribution
- Change price
- Change promotion
- Change the use of the product
- Change the name of the product
- Add extension lines

(c) (i) Job description – states the title of the job, tasks, duties, responsibilities and location. Work conditions may also be included, e.g. holiday entitlement benefits and working hours. **4**

(ii) **4**
- Appraisal allows a discussion to take place between the employee and their line manager.
- The discussion covers the employee's past performance and identifies strengths and weaknesses.
- Weaknesses may be addressed by training.
- The employee's development may also be discussed, which can be aided by training.

(d) (i) **6**
- Employers have a duty of care towards employees and must provide safe working conditions and insist on safe working practices.
- Employees have a duty to take reasonable care of their own health and safety as well as that of other employees.
- Credit contents of Act which employers have to provide, e.g. washing facilities

(ii) **4**
- Financial costs of modifying product to meet terms of law
- Production may be banned
- Taxation may be increased affecting cash flow
- Information may have to be shared

(25)

Marks

11 *(a)*
- Sales maximisation– an organisation aims to maximise the revenue generated from sales. **6**
- Social responsibility – an organisation aims to project a good image and be responsible towards its customers.
- Profit maximisation – an organisation aims to maximise its profits.

(b)
- Reduced risk of business failure **6**
- Less financial risk
- Can introduce new products as old products go into decline to maintain a healthy portfolio
- May be less productive in the long term compared to merger
- May still be costly to the organisation
- May lose out on additional expertise from the merged company

(c) (i)
- Primary information – from an original source. **4**
- Secondary information – from a secondary published source.
- Internal information – gathered from the organisation's internal records.
- External information – gathered from sources outside the organisation.

(ii) Good information is: **5**
- Timely
- Accurate
- Objective and free from bias
- Concise
- Appropriate
- Available
- Complete
- Cost-effective
- High quality
- Relevant

(d)
- SWOT analysis – strengths, weaknesses, opportunities, threats. **4**
- Involves identification of the problem, identification of the objectives, identification of the constraints and the gathering of information.
- Managers can use SWOT analysis to make informed decisions that are not rushed and follow a logical process. Time will also have been taken to develop alternative solutions.

(25)

Marks

12 *(a)* (i) Profit and loss account: **6**

- To show income and costs and work out if the business has run at a profit or a loss
- Calculated over a period of time, usually one year

Balance sheet:

- Shows the value of the business on a particular date
- Lists the assets and liabilities of the business and how the business is financed

(ii) Liquidity is a measure of how much cash a business has available at a particular point in time, and how it manages its cashflow. Cashflow is important to all businesses as they must manage receipts and payments of cash, and ensure that the business has enough cash to operate on a day-to-day basis. This also includes anticipating periods where cash will be in short supply, or managing/investing cash surpluses. **5**

(b) Gross profit percentage **6**

- Measures the profit made from buying and selling stock
- Changes in this ratio may result from changes in supplier prices

Net profit percentage

- Measures how much profit has been made after all business expenses have been taken into account
- Changes may result from changes in the gross profit percentage or from changes in the selling price

Current Ratio

- Shows the ability of a business to pay its short-term debts
- Should normally be in the region of 2:1
- If this ratio is too high, it may indicate that funds employed in the business could be better invested elsewhere

(c) (i) Span of control is the term used to describe the number of employees who work under a manager or supervisor. The span of control (i.e. the number of employees under the manager) will be dependent on a variety of factors, including the experience of the manager, the task to be undertaken and capability of the employees working for the manager. **4**

Organisation culture is the term used to describe the values, beliefs and normal working practices in place within an organisation. This should be shared with all staff.

(ii) Senior management within an organisation are responsible for: **4**

- Strategic and tactical decision-making
- Promoting and developing the organisation
- Setting long-term goals for the organisation
- Managing other managers

(25)

Marks

13 *(a)* (i)
- Able to cope with unexpected changes in demand. **6**
- Orders have to be made less frequently which saves administration costs and time.
- Bulk buying discounts may be available for buying in bulk.

- High costs – storage, maintenance, security, insurance.
- Outflow of cash which could be used better elsewhere.
- Takes up a lot of space.
- May deteriorate or become obsolete.

(ii) Stock has to be paid for (outflow) and does not bring any money in until it is sold. This may be many months after the stock is paid for and may cause a shortage of cash. **2**

Holding stock may mean that the stock has been purchased at a lower price and benefits the cashflow position. This could be due to bulk buying discounts, or storing goods at a lower price than if purchasing just in time.

(b) Branded goods **6**
- Command a higher price for the supermarket.
- Consumers perceive the goods to be of higher quality.
- Consumers become brand loyal.
- Supermarket will be able to sell other goods produced by the manufacturer of the branded product on its reputation.
- Consumers enjoy the image of using brand products.
- Manufacturers pay for a lot of the promotion.

Own label
- Supermarkets may have a higher mark up on these products.
- Cheaper for the consumer.
- Increases choice for the consumer.

(c)
- Identify why there is such a high staff turnover, possibly by interviewing staff and supervisors. **3**
- Rectify the problem – improve working conditions/pay.
- Implement recruitment process.

(d) (ii)
- Check application forms/CV against person specification to select suitable candidates for a vacancy. **5**
- Check references.
- Draw up a short list of those suitable to interview.
- Testing may take place.
- Interview.

(ii) Ensure that working conditions and pay are satisfactory or better than those offered by competitors. **3**
- Provide adequate training.
- Offer perks such as discount on purchasing, sports facilities, etc.
- Ensure that an attractive promotion structure exists.

(25)

Marks

14 *(a)* (i) Market research will help the organisation identify: **4**

- Who their customers are
- How much consumers will pay
- What consumers would like in the future
- The current market situation
- And test new products

(ii)

- Interview – researcher asks a series of set questions and can help clarify questions for the interviewee. **3**
- Questionnaire – set questions on a form with answers filled in by the respondent.
- Test marketing – launch the product on a small part of the market and use the consumers' comments to make improvements if needed.
- Consumer panels – small groups of consumers brought together to get their views on a product.

(b)

- They can provide a high degree of personal service. **4**
- Responsive to the customers' needs.
- Customer loyalty can be built up.

- Duplication of some functional areas will be necessary.
- Higher staff costs.
- Can be more difficult to control.

(c) The organisation **8**

- Can provide a wider range of products.
- No need to open more shops.
- Reaches a much wider market.
- It is a fast-growing market.
- Can sell to consumers directly in their home.

The consumer

- A much wider choice of products and suppliers.
- May get the product cheaper.
- No need to leave home.
- No travel or parking charges.
- Deliveries are made directly to the consumer's home.

(d)

- Allowing debtors too long to pay – sell invoices to debt factoring company or bank. **6**
- Too much money tied up in stock – introduce a just-in-time system of stock control.
- Expenses getting out of control – set and control budgets.
- Low product demand – change marketing mix (e.g. offer discounts) to encourage sales.

(25)

Marks

15 *(a)* (i) Marketing **6**

- Databases could be compiled with consumer information.
- Websites could be set up to sell products online.
- Spreadsheets could be used to forecast demand.

(ii) Operations

- Spreadsheets could be used to prepare production budgets.
- Databases could be set up with supplier details.
- Automatic ordering could be set up using the internet to connect to suppliers.

(iii) Finance

- Spreadsheets can be used to record financial transactions.
- Spreadsheets can be used to carry out 'what if' analysis.
- Networks will allow automatic updating of accounts.

(b) (i) **3**

- Make staff redundant to reduce costs.
- Increase selling price if market allows.
- Seek cheaper suppliers.
- Reduce budget levels to departments to control spending.

(ii) **3**

- Redundancies may harm the image of the business, which may conflict with corporate responsibility.
- Increasing prices may interfere with the objective of sales maximisation.
- Cheaper suppliers may not offer the quality needed for producing high quality goods for consumer satisfaction.
- Reducing budgets may affect the ability to increase market share.

(c) (i) **4**

- Allows production to be customised for the consumer.
- Workers can be more motivated as they can use creative skills.
- Easier to organise production.

- It is more expensive as it does not benefit from economies of scale.
- Output levels will be low.
- It is labour-intensive and labour costs will be high due to skill level.

(ii) **6**

- Quality can be designed and planned into the production process so that it works well.
- Quality materials can be used.
- Reliable suppliers should be sought.
- Staff can be trained to a high standard to ensure quality output.
- They can use quality assurance procedures so that faults are identified at an early stage.
- Products do not move to the next stage unless they meet the standards set.
- Storage facilities should allow the products to be stored safely.
- Packaging should be designed to adequately protect the product in transit.

(d) **3**

- The PR department may deal with customer complaints.
- They will deal with bad publicity from the media.
- They may issue recall notices to customers.
- They may arrange compensation payments if necessary.

(25)

Marks

16 *(a)* Training is carried out at a different location from the employee's place of work, e.g. training centre or college. **4**

- Specialist trainers deliver the training.
- Worker will not be called away to answer telephone, for example.
- Specialist equipment may be available.

(b) Staff training **6**

- Produces more productive workers which increases profitability
- Produces more confident and efficient workers
- Creates a more flexible workforce
- Allows change to be introduced more easily
- Increases job satisfaction
- Increases worker motivation which leads to increased production
- Reduces accidents and injuries
- Improves the image of the organisation
- Improves the employee's chances of promotion

(c) (i) Flow **8**

- Costs are spread over a large number of items, therefore the unit cost is reduced.
- Bulk discounts are likely to be gained when purchasing.
- Huge quantities can be produced.
- Automated process lowers labour costs.

- Huge investment needed to set up process.
- Individual customer requirements cannot be met.
- Equipment may not be suitable for more than one purpose.
- Worker motivation low due to repetitive process.

(ii) Job

- One-off orders can be produced to meet the needs of the customer.
- A high price may be charged.
- Process can be adapted to meet customer need even once the process is started.
- Workers are more likely to be motivated as work is varied and requires skill.
- Supervision can be easily carried out.

- Expensive process due to high skill of staff required.
- High costs as they are not spread over large output.
- A wide variety of equipment may be needed.

(d) A quality assurance process should be established. This is where standards are set, agreed and met throughout the organisation. **7**

- Process is based on the prevention of errors, not finding them.
- Checking takes place throughout the process.
- Quality raw materials and equipment are essential.
- Monitoring and controlling of whole system essential.
- Commitment and skill of workforce must be high.
- Aim for perfection.
- Delivery deadlines met.
- After-sales service provided.
- Customers' needs considered.

(25)

				Marks
17	*(a)*	(i)	By employing quality assurance and control measures in the production process, such as benchmarking, quality control, quality circles, total quality management and adherence to British quality standards.	**4**
		(ii)	• Benchmarking – involves identifying and copying the best practice used by another organisation. The aim is to improve quality. • Quality circles – involves small groups of workers meeting at regular intervals to discuss improvements in the quality process. They report back to management who then decide on a course of action.	**5**
	(b)	(i)	• High costs of building/insurance • Theft/pilferage • If warehouse facilities are centralised, distribution costs may be increased • Fire or water damage may result in a huge loss of stock	**4**
		(ii)	• Accounts for over 80 per cent of goods transported in the UK • Road network more extensive than the rail network • Quick and cost-effective to use • Door-to-door delivery is possible	**3**
	(c)		Decentralised structure differs from centralised structure: • Control and decision-making delegated to individual departments • Faster decision-making • Subordinates are given more responsibility for making decisions • Marks should also be awarded for justification.	**5**
	(d)		Budgets aid the monitoring and control of costs as they allow production of a forecast to estimate future costs and spending. This allows periods of particularly high or low costs to be identified and appropriate action to be planned. Budget targets can also be set to control costs with penalties if the targets are not met.	**4**
				(25)

SOLUTIONS

Marks

18 *(a)*
- Sole trader retains profits; plc issues dividends. **4**
- Sole trader makes all decisions; Board of Directors control and shareholders vote.
- Sole trader financed by owners' savings, plc financed by shares.
- Sole trader easy to set up; plc must abide by Companies Act.

(b) (i)
- Bank loan – relatively easy to obtain and allows payments to be spread. **2**
- Owners' savings – allows owners to keep control.

(ii)
- Risk of failure reduced. **5**
- Provided with the business idea.
- May be given training.
- Franchiser may advertise nationally.
- The business may already be established in the market.

(c)
- Borrowing. **5**
- Discounts offered to encourage fast payment.
- Encourage cash payments by discounting or promotion.
- Sell unneeded assets.
- Arrange credit suppliers.

(d) (i)
- Decisions made by people at the centre of the organisation. **2**
- Staff are told what to do by the entrepreneur.

(ii) Hierarchical **7**
- Tall with many layers of management.
- Long chain of command.
- Decisions and instructions passed down; information passed up.
- Communication may be slow.

Flat
- Few layers of management.
- Short chain of command
- Decisions made more quickly

(maximum of 2 marks for correct diagrams)

(25)

Marks

19 *(a)*
- This is an example of vertical integration. **3**
- Two organisations that operate at the same stage in the production process join together.
- Removes a competitor from the market.
- Allows the organisation to grow quickly, acquiring new assets and customers.

(b) (i)
- The ability of managers to manage the change. **4**
- The finance available to ensure that the takeover was successful.
- Marketing, including product range and distribution process.
- The willingness of staff to accept the change.
- The number and skills of the workforce.

(ii)
- Problems could be identified at an early stage. **6**
- Objectives could be agreed to allow all staff to work to same goals.
- The information gathered would give a full picture of the current situation.
- The information would be analysed thoroughly.
- A range of solutions would be devised, so that when things started to go wrong, alternative actions could be taken which would achieve the objectives.
- Communication of the decision and the objectives would be made to all staff so that they were all aware of what was happening.
- The progress of the decision would be monitored and controlled to ensure success.

(c) (i)
- They could adopt a low price strategy where they charge lower prices than their competitors. **6**
- The could set a market price where they charge similar prices to their competitors.
- They could use a high price strategy to infer a higher level of quality than their competitors.
- They could use penetration pricing – setting a low price until market share is gained.
- They could use destroyer pricing – setting an artificially low price until competition leaves the market.
- The could use promotional pricing – lowering the price short in the term to create new interest in their shops.

(ii)
- They could advertise on television, although very expensive. **6**
- They can target market segments by having adverts during particular programmes.
- They could use newspaper adverts, though national papers are expensive.
- Newspapers can be read again and again.
- Billboards are cheaper and have a high impact.
- They may not reach the target audience, and have to be in suitable places.
- Local radio could be used which would be relatively cheap.
- They would need frequently repeated adverts to reach their target audience.

(25)

Marks

20 *(a)* (i) Budgets **4**

- Financial plans for the coming months/years.
- Managers have to remain within budget.
- Ensures any excess spending is highlighted early.

Ratio analysis

- Liquidity ratios highlight trends within the business.
- Current Ratio shows how able the business is to meet its short-term debts.
- Acid test ratio shows the same but without stock, the least liquid current asset.

(ii)
- Selling shares on the stock market. It can raise large sums of money that do not have to be paid back. **6**
- Obtaining a loan from the bank. Will raise large amounts of money that can be paid back in instalments over a long period of time.
- Selling off unwanted assets or parts of the business. Can raise large amounts of money without having to give up any control of the business, and it does not have to be repaid.
- Borrow money from venture capitalists. You can obtain large sums of money when the banks think it is too risky. They will often provide additional business expertise.

(b) (i)
- Decisions on stock levels will be made at the planning stage. **6**
- Should set an economic stock level which ensures that production is not interrupted.
- Economic level should also ensure that stock levels are kept as low as possible to avoid costs.
- The minimum stock level will make sure that there is always stock for production, allowing for delivery times.
- The re-order stock level is set to ensure that new stock arrives before they run out.
- Should make allowance for unexpected delays in delivery.
- The re-order stock quantity is the amount needed to bring the level back to the economic stock level.

(ii)
- Requires very good relationship with suppliers. **4**
- Reliance on suppliers may make the organisation vulnerable to stoppages in production.
- This could mean poor customer service.
- Difficult to deal with unexpected increases in demand.
- Could lead to a loss of customers if they cannot get what they want from the business.

(c)
- The type of product – highly technical products use a direct channel. Premium products will only be sold through selected outlets. **5**
- The market – small local markets use a direct channel. Mass markets use both wholesalers and retailers.
- Legal requirements – certain products can only be sold at licensed/approved outlets.
- Buying habits – consumers will expect to be able to buy certain products in certain places, so manufacturers have to use these outlets (e.g. garden centres)
- The business – some organisations like Boots manufacture, distribute and have their own retails outlets.

(25)

Marks

21 *(a)* (i)
- Difficult to reach many people they might wish to, as there is not a mobile phone directory, and email addresses might not be known by the organisation. **4**
- Staff require training to use the technology efficiently.
- Cost of purchasing equipment.
- Not all potential customers have access to email.
- May not be able to target the appropriate market segment this way (older people may not use text messaging or email as frequently as a younger market).

(ii)
- Encouraging people to enter competitions where they leave their mobile number or email address allows organisation to gather these details, along with some personal information about the user. **4**
- Purchasing online may give the consumer price discounts – their details are left once logged on.
- Free gift etc if purchasing online.

(b) (i)
- Customers may believe they are receiving a better quality product or service. **3**
- Customers like to be seen using products which carry a superior image, and buy more frequently (snob value).
- Employees are associated with working for a business with a good image – they become motivated.
- Shareholders should benefit from higher dividends as the quality image pays off in increased sales/profits.

(ii) To improve profitability **6**
- Promotional techniques aim to increase sales in order to achieve this.
- Discount pricing should increase volume of sales and hence profitability.
- Changing the place where the product is sold may increase sales volume and therefore profitability.

To enter a new market segment
- Promotional techniques can be aimed specifically at the market segment to encourage purchasing

To provide a service
- A charity may use promotional materials (leaflets, stickers, etc) to increase donations made which would allow them to carry out this objective.

(c) (i)
- Budgets allow managers to plan: the quantity and value of sales; the quantity to be produced; the amount of resources required; the amount of cash which will be available. **5**
- There is a link between the different budgets, e.g. the amount of planned sales influences the amount of goods to be produced and the resources required.
- Allows target-setting for staff, which can increase motivation.
- Allows remedial action to be taken, e.g. cut costs, increase income, arrange borrowing in the case of a cash budget.
- Allows better use of money to be made if surplus cash is projected (investment).
- Makes manager accountable for operating their budget.

Marks

(ii)
- Marketing departments may require cash in order to carry out promotional activities, e.g. advertising or free gifts. **3**
- Marketing may wish to discount pricing, which reduces cash inflow in the short term.
- Marketing may wish to use techniques such as buy one, get one free, which reduces income.
- Finance departments may not wish to lay out so much cash in order to take more in at a later date.
- Finance department may wish to reduce the amount spent on overheads.

(25)

Marks

22 *(a)*
- Strategic – a long term decision made by senior management which affects the overaall aims of the organisation. E.g. to increase profitability **6**
- Tactical – a medium term decision taken by middle management in order to achieve the strategic decisions. E.g. increase promotion.
- Operational – a day to day decision taken by departmental managers. E.g. to change staff duty rota.

(b)
- Information can be posted on the intranet on a regular basis. **4**
- The information is not available outside the organisation.
- All staff have access to the same information.
- Information can be stored and recalled time and time again.

(c) (i)
- Primary – gained first hand by e.g. market research. **2**
- Secondary – already gathered for another purpose.
- Internal – information held within the organisation.
- External – information available from newspapers, Internet etc.

(ii) Internal **6**
- Accurate information.
- Records can be used to show past performance and targets then set.
- Costs involved in producing records
- Takes time to build up information.

External
- Useful to know about PESTEC factors.
- Time consuming and expensive to gather.
- May be out of date.
- Available to competitors.
- May be biased.

(d) Marketing **7**
- Will decide on an appropriate price.
- Will promote product to encourage sales.
- Will ensure the product is sold in an appropriate place.
- Will make sure the product is what the customer wants.

Research and Development
- Ensures the organisation makes the products which will be demanded in the future.
- Look constantly to inprove.
- Look to invent new products.

(25)

SOLUTIONS

Marks

23 *(a)* (i)
- Sole trader – a one person organisation with unlimited liability. **6**
- Partnership – a two or more person organisation who control the business together. Controlled by a partnership agreement, stating the rights of each partner.
- Private limited company – a company whose shares are privately owned by a minimum of one shareholder. Run by a director or directors – must be a minimum of one director, and a company secretary.
- Public limited company – a company whose shares are available to trade on the stock market. Must be a minimum of two shareholders and £50,000 capital.

(ii)
- Profit maximisation – exists in the private sector where a company aims to make as much profit as possible. **6**
- Sales maximisation – to achieve as many sales as possible and maximise revenue. This is popular with people who work on a commission basis.
- Social responsibility – to ensure that the organisation has a good public image and is appealing to its customers. This includes having a responsible and fair attitude in dealing with suppliers and impact on the environment.

(b)
- Owners – make decisions about how the business is run. **6**
- Shareholders – influence the operation of the business by voting for particular directors.
- Managers – make important decisions which may affect the business both positively and negatively.
- Government – policies and legislation can impact on business.
- Customers – can contribute to product development and decide whether or not to purchase the company's products.

(c)
- Grievance procedure – every organisation should have a grievance procedure. It should outline the process to be followed where an employee feels that he/she has suffered discrimination, harassment or victimisation. **4**
- Arbitration – this is used when a dispute cannot be settled amicably. An independent third party, e.g. ACAS, may be brought in to give an impartial solution to the problem to which both parties agree.

(d)
- Equal Pay Act 1970 – to ensure that all employees receive the same rate of pay where work of equal value is undertaken. **3**
- Sex Discrimination Act 1975 – ensures that there is no discrimination on the grounds of sex or marriage.
- Disability Discrimination Act 1995 – ensures that there is no discrimination against disabled people.
- Race Relations Act 1976 – prohibits discrimination on the grounds of race, nationality, colour or ethnic origin.
- Employment Equality (Religion or Belief) Regulations 2003 – prohibits discrimination on the grounds of religion or belief.

(25)

Marks

24 *(a)* (i)
- Working time is lost while the employee is away being trained. **3**
- Other staff have to cover, increasing their workload.
- This could lead to inefficiencies and/or customer complaints.
- Employees will find it easier to get a better job and leave.

(ii)
- It will increase the competence of the workforce. **3**
- It improves staff flexibility.
- It will be easier to introduce necessary changes.
- Production levels will increase.

(b) (i) The retailer **4**
- Dealer loaders, where the retailer is given six boxes for the price of five.
- Point of sale display such as display racks.
- Sale or return where if they do not sell the product, they can return it without cost.
- Training for sales staff so that they are fully aware of the product.
- Extended credit where they have longer to pay for the goods.

(ii) The customer **4**
- They could use advertising.
- They could use promotional offers, e.g. ten per cent extra free.
- They could offer price discounts.
- They could use a celebrity to endorse their products.
- They could use sponsorship of an event.

(c)
- New products allow them to replace products before they go into decline. **6**
- They can attract new markets or market segments to their products.
- It will allow them to gain a competitive edge over their rivals.
- It may allow them to hold a monopoly position for a period of time.
- It allows them to meet changing consumer demand.
- It allows them to reduce the level of risk by freshening up the product range.

(d)
- They could carry out a survey, with interviewers asking a set of questions of consumers. **5**
- The survey could be carried out in the street, or over the phone.
- They could issue questionnaires with a set of questions that the consumers answer themselves.
- This could be issued in store or through the post.
- They could use a consumer panel, made up of small groups of consumers, and ask their opinions.
- They could study market research data on trends in their market.
- They could refer to trade magazines to find out what developments there are in the market.

(25)

			Marks
25 *(a)* (i)	• A job description is a description of the job vacancy stating the title, location, tasks, duties and responsibilities of the post. • An application form is completed by the job applicant to detail their personal details, qualifications and experience in relation to the vacancy. • A person specification details the type of person that would be suitable to fill the vacant post. It describes the qualifications, experience, personal qualities and interests that the ideal candidate would possess.		**6**
(ii)	• Aptitude tests – used to assess the natural characteristics possessed by an applicant. The test will often reflect the skills required to carry out the job. • Psychometric tests – used to assess personalities and traits, usually by means of a series of questions with no right or wrong answers. Justification for use should also be provided.		**6**
(b)	• Freedom of Information (Scotland) Act 2002 – gives a right of access to all recorded information held by Scottish public authorities covered by the Act. • Disability Discrimination Act 2005 – aims to improve the rights of disabled people.		**6**
(c) (i)	• Access to a new and larger market • May attract incentives from the government • May be the only supplier of that product in that country • May be able to charge higher prices in the export country		**4**
(ii)	Grant		**1**
(iii)	• Sales maximisation – to achieve as much sales revenue as possible. • Profit maximisation – to make as much profit as possible.		**2**
			(25)

SOLUTIONS

Marks

26 *(a)* (i)
- Qualitative information is information expressed in words. It is descriptive and may include opinions or judgements. **4**
- Quantitative information is information that can be measured and is usually expressed in numerical format.

(ii) Primary information: **5**
- First-hand information
- Correct for purpose
- May be difficult to gather
- May be expensive to source

Secondary information:
- Usually inexpensive
- Wide variety of information available
- May be out of date
- Is also available to the competition

(b) (i)
- Email – essential for modern business communication; instant, cost-effective. **6**
- Computer network – essential to the operation of most modern businesses; information can be shared across the network, files can be stored centrally.
- Videoconferencing – enables people in different locations to have a meeting without the need to travel; saves on travel and meeting costs.
- Internet and e-commerce – vast amounts of information can be sourced and communicated to customers; e-commerce allows businesses to sell products and services online and worldwide, allowing costs to be cut.

(ii) Organisations have to meet the eight principles of the Data Protection Act 1998 in relation to the collection and storage of personal information held: **4**
- Fairly and lawfully processed
- Processed for limited purposes
- Adequate, relevant, and not excessive
- Accurate
- Not kept for longer than necessary
- Processed in accordance with the data subject's rights
- Secure
- Not transferred to countries without adequate protection

(c) (i)
- Aptitude tests – used to assess the natural characteristics possessed by an applicant. The test will often reflect the skills required to carry out the job. **4**
- Psychometric tests – used to assess personalities and traits, usually by means of a series of questions with no right or wrong answers.

(ii) Organisations may use the services of a recruitment agency to source new staff for the following reasons: **2**
- May be a specialised position for which an agency will have access to more suitable applicants.
- To save money.
- The organisation may not have the necessary experience within the human resources department to recruit for the vacancy.

(25)

Marks

27 *(a)* (i) When a firm takes control of another firm **1**

(ii) Shareholders may be offered cash to purchase their shares. If they agree to the price offered, they receive the cash and are no longer shareholders with any control over the organisation. If they choose to remain as shareholders they may find that the newly formed business may be more profitable and increase their dividends. The opposite is also possible. **6**

Customers may notice little difference if the firm continues to operate in the same way under the original name. However, products offered may differ as the firm taking over may put their own products in the stores. They might also close branches down, which makes shopping less convenient for the customer.

Employees will have new employers who may run the firm in a different way. Job losses may occur due to streamlining and removal of the duplication of tasks between the two firms.

(b) (i)
- Gross profit ratio shows the profit made from each pound of sales. Expressed as a percentage, improvements or reductions in the percentage from year to year can easily be seen. **4**
- Net profit ratio shows the profit made from sales after the expenses have been deducted.

(ii)
- Future developments may increase profitability, but the effects will not yet be seen in the final accounts. **3**
- The current figures may be an exceptionally bad year, e.g. during a recession, and performance will improve.

(c)
- Reducing price may help regain market share, but it will be necessary to sell more products to make up for the cut in price. **5**
- Reducing price will possibly be short term as competitors will probably match it or even undercut the price.
- Advertising can draw attention to the product and encourage consumers to buy.
- Buy one, get one free, free gift with purchase, etc will encourage consumers to buy.
- It will be necessary to find out why the consumers are buying from the competitors, and match or better their offer.

(d) (i)
- Computers allow stock records to be updated quickly when receipts and issues are made, by scanning a barcode. **6**
- They can be programmed to reorder as soon as the reorder level is reached.
- Managers can use the computer to identity best-selling products and make sure they stock more of them, and drop any non-movers

(ii) Too much stock means that an organisation has high costs – maintenance, storage, security, insurance etc. A large amount of space is taken up. Cash has to be spent which may be put to better use elsewhere. Stock can be stolen, damaged or go out of date before it is used.

Too little stock means that an organisation is unable to cope with unexpected demands. Production may be held up. Customers not receiving goods may purchase elsewhere and never return. Administration costs will rise if stock has to be reordered.

(25)

Marks

28 *(a)* • The quality of materials will be reflected in the final product for the consumers. **4**
- The quality of the workforce will affect how well the products are made.
- The quality and reliability of machinery will affect the level of wastage and quality of final output.
- High quality will reduce the number of returns and complaints from customers.

(b) *(i)* • Job analysis is carried out to see what vacancy exists. **8**
- It looks at the main physical and mental elements of the job, specific skills required and responsibilities.
- Job description drawn up with overall purpose of the job and main tasks.
- Job description can be used as a basis for the job advert, and help applicants decide if they should apply.
- Person specification is drawn up to identify the individual who would be best suited for the job.
- It would include the desirable physical attributes, skills, qualifications and experience.
- The organisation must decide whether to recruit internally and/or externally.
- Application forms should be sent out, allowing comparison of responses to the same set of questions.
- The most suitable people should then be invited to interview, with appropriate testing if required.

(ii) • Staff training and development should take place. **4**
- Induction training should be offered for new staff.
- A continuous process of training should be carried out to keep skills up to date.
- Training will allow all workers to achieve the level of performance of the most experienced workers.
- Appraisal should be carried out to identify training needs.

(c) • Quality standards are recognised by suppliers and customers. **6**
- Waste will be reduced.
- Customer complaints and returns will be reduced.
- The reputation of the organisation will be improved.
- Quality assurance will allow standards to be set in the operations process, reducing the need for management intervention.

- The organisation must invest in the quality assurance system – cost.
- Staff training must be a continuing process – cost.
- All employees must be committed to the system.

(d) • Kite mark – shows that the product meets certain safety standards. **3**
- Association of British Travel Agents (ABTA) – will protect customers should the travel agent go into liquidation/bankruptcy, and provides other protection.
- Investors in People – the organisation has a commitment to staff training and development.
- CE mark – an EU mark given to products who meet certain standards.

(25)

Marks

29 *(a)* Pricing strategies such as: **5**

- Penetration pricing
- Destroyer pricing
- Competitive pricing
- Market skimming

Promotional strategies may involve reducing prices for a short period of time, often to attract new interest in a product or to reduce stock levels, the use of advertising and public relations exercises.

(b) Niche marketing is the identification of a gap in the market and the aiming of a specific product at a small market segment. Volkswagen might try to market their car by using advertising campaigns, targeting the customers most likely to want to buy the car. **4**

(c) (i) Flow production is a process where production moves continuously from one operation to the next. In the case of car production, cars move along a production line with parts being added at each stage until a finished product leaves the factory. **2**

(ii) Quality management is important to an organisation such as Volkswagen because: **5**

- It will affect their reputation.
- They must ensure that quality is right first time to minimise costs.

(d) (i) **5**

- Cash is essential for the day-to-day running of the organisation.
- Poor liquidity means that the organisation may not have enough cash to operate.
- Poor liquidity means that the organisation may not be able to meet its short-term debts.
- Cashflow management involves managing the cash in the organisation so that periods of cash shortages can be identified in advance.

  Effective cashflow management means that the business should never run short of cash in the short term.

(ii) The liquidity ratios are the current ratio and the acid test ratio. These are calculated to show the ability of the organisation to meet its short term debts. Once calculated, the ratios can be compared with previous years in the organisation, or compared with other organisations operating in the same sector. **4**

(25)

Marks

30 *(a)*
- Customers may be interested in profits as they may feel they are paying too much. **4**
- Customers may wish to be sure the company is to keep trading.
- Shareholders wish to know how good their investment is.
- Shareholders may wish to buy more or sell their existing shares.

(b) (i)
- Offer specialist advice. **4**
- Promotions.
- Hold stock that is not available anywhere else e.g. imports.
- Project a more upmarket image.
- Match or undercut price.
- Offer after sales service/guarantee.

(ii)
- Save time and travelling expenses. **4**
- Goods can be delivered to the home address.
- Wider choice of some goods.
- Price competitive.
- Know immediately if goods are in stock.

(c) (i)
- Application forms and CVs received. **5**
- Application forms and CVs checked against Person Specification.
- Check references.
- Interviews.
- Tests.

(ii)
- Training for new staff. **4**
- Covers information about the organisation and its policies.
- Allows employee to meet colleagues.
- Makes employee feel welcome.
- Makes employee aware of how the company operates as a whole.

(d)
- Comparisons can be made with similar firms. **4**
- Comparisons can be made with previous years.
- Highlights trends.
- Helps with decision making when differences in performance are shown up.

(25)

SOLUTIONS

Marks

31 *(a)* (i)
- Gross profit – profit before taking into account business expenses. **6**
- Cashflow statement – shows the movement of cash in and out of the business over a financial year.
- Budget – a list of planned expenses over a set period of time.

(ii)
- Financial instability **4**
- Possible failure of the organisation
- Inability to plan for the future
- Inability to pay short-term debts

(iii) Short-term finance: **6**
- Trade credit
- Overdraft
- Short-term bank loan

Long-term finance:
- Long-term bank loan
- Share issue
- Debentures

Justification for each method of finance identified must be provided.

(b) Following a takeover, organisational structure may change, e.g. from a flat to a hierarchical structure, from a centralised structure to a decentralised structure. **4**

Organisational culture may change involve delayering (cutting out levels of management to flatten the structure) or downsizing (removing certain areas of the organisation's activities to cut costs and improve efficiency).

(c) (i)
- National organisations operate within one country. **5**
- International organisations operate within at least two different countries, with their head office based in one country.
- Multinational organisations operate across several countries, with main offices in each country.

(ii) Multinationals may hold a competitive advantage for the following reasons:
- Governments in other countries may offer incentives such as tax concessions or large grants to entice them to open there.
- Lower wage rates may make the cost of production much lower.
- Higher skilled workers may be available for the same or lower cost.
- Legislation in other countries may be more relaxed, meaning production can be much cheaper (working hours, environmental restrictions, minimum wage, building regulations, etc).
- The rate of corporation tax may be lower, which means they can keep more of their profits.
- The business can then operate competitively in the local market.

(25)

Marks

32 *(a)*
- Political – levels of taxation, supplies allowed by producing countries. **6**
- Economic – market price of crude oil, cost of exploration.
- Social – cars owned per household, increase in air travel
- Technological – advances in alternative fuels/power, introduction of more efficient engines.
- Environmental – effects on global warming, environmental legislation.
- Competitive – price competition between suppliers.

(b)
- Public relations is the way that the organisation communicates with the external environment at a corporate level. **5**
- These are planned communications by the organisation to enhance its image.
- They would communicate this way with the press, government, shareholders and other stakeholders.
- Can involve issuing press releases, press conferences, making charitable donations, sponsorship and product endorsement.
- In some organisations the customer services/care department will be included in public relations.
- Sometimes referred to as corporate communications.

(c)
- They can keep up with market trends. **6**
- Will ensure that new products will not fail.
- Can give them a competitive edge.
- Can make improvements in quality.
- Can make improvements in product safety.
- May give them a monopoly position until competitors produce new products.
- Will enhance the image of the organisation.

(d)
- Allows business to concentrate on core activities. **8**
- Business no longer has to staff or accommodate the function.
- Allows the organisation to employ specialists.
- Specialist firm may produce at lower cost.
- Specialist firm may have specialist equipment/be more efficient.

- Will lose control of that part of their business.
- Specialist firm may not meet standards required.
- Communication problems between the firms may arise.
- Success depends on very good relationships between the businesses.
- Confidential information may have to be shared with the specialist company.

(25)

Marks

33 *(a)* (i)
- The trading account shows the gross profit. **6**
- It shows the profit made on buying and selling products.
- Gross profit is calculated by deducting the cost of goods sold from sales revenue.
- The profit and loss account shows how much net profit the business has made.
- The net profit is calculated by deducting expenses from the gross profit.
- The balance sheet shows the financial worth of the organisation.
- It includes assets liabilities and capital.

(ii)
- Suppliers – can increase or decrease prices, credit terms or delivery times. **6**
- Managers – the effectiveness of their decisions will affect how well the organisation achieves its objectives.
- Government – changes in legislation or economic policy may force change in the business.
- Customers – can decide whether or not to buy the products.

(b) (i)
- Plcs would want to maximise the amount of profit they make from their investment. **4**
- A charity would want to maximise the amount of money they can raise to help their cause.
- A plc may adopt an objective of corporate responsibility to improve their image with stakeholders.
- A charity would also want to create a good image as they also have to compete for donations with other charities.

(ii)
- They can obtain money from the government to help with their cause. **4**
- They may come to rely on that money, but changing political and economic forces may see it reduced or withdrawn.
- They can convince people to sign up to make monthly donations.
- There has been a lot of bad publicity about charities methods in trying to convince people to do this.
- They can advertise for donations on television.
- The adverts are expensive and the money could be better used elsewhere.

(c)
- Management have to plan – make strategic decisions for the charity, setting objectives. **5**
- They have to co-ordinate limited resources in order to achieve those objectives.
- They have to make sure that all staff know what to do, and are working to the same objectives.
- They have to monitor performance to ensure that the objectives are going to be achieved.
- They have to change plans when external factors change their situation.
- They have to motivate both staff and volunteers in order to achieve the objectives.

(25)

Marks

34 *(a)* (i) Demand **5**

- Increase or decrease production accordingly.

Competition

- Increase or decrease prices.
- Offer promotions to attract customers.

Changes in technology

- Organise staff training.
- Invest in new equipment.

Structure of the labour market

- Employ more temporary staff.
- Use recruitment agencies to source new staff.

(ii) Horizontal integration is the term used to describe two organisations who produce the same type of product or provide the same type of service, coming together. Advantages include cost savings and cheaper prices to consumers. Disadvantages include domination of the market and eventual higher prices for consumers. **5**

Vertical integration occurs where organisations at different stages of production in the same industry come together, e.g. an oil company integrating with petrol retailers. Advantages include increased profits and better control. Disadvantages include difficulties in integrating staff in the new business, and a lack of control of all parts of the business.

(iii) **3**

- Concentrate on core activities
- Raise finance
- Cut costs
- Increase efficiency

(b) (i) **5**

- Lack of knowledge of financial position at any point in time
- Lack of ability to plan for the future
- Lack of ability to recognise period of cash shortages or cash surpluses
- Unable to set/measure targets
- Unable to accurately forecast functional budgets

(ii) **4**

- Gross profit percentage – measures the profit from buying and selling stock.
- Net profit percentage – measures the profit made after the business has paid all expenses.
- Return on capital employed – measures the return on capital invested in the business by the owner/shareholders.

(c) **3**

- Staff divided into divisions with a regional focus.
- Allows tailoring of services to customers in each area.
- Allows the business to compete in regional markets.

(25)

Marks

35 *(a)* Lenders **6**

- Expect to have their loans returned
- Expect to have interest paid on a regular basis

Employees

- Expect good working conditions and pay
- Look for job security, promotion prospects, etc

Customers

- Look for value for money
- Look for quality products

(b)
- Questionnaires – a list of questions could be asked by telephone, internet or post. The people could be asked what they like and dislike about the product. **4**
- Consumer panels – where a group of people are gathered together to sample and give opinions on the products. Feedback is gathered immediately.
- Observation – consumers can be observed by a person or camera. This allows their shopping habits to be seen. This may identify poor display of goods etc.

(c)
- No rash decisions are made as time is taken to gather information and analyse the situation. **5**
- Decisions are made using knowledge of facts and information that has been gathered.
- Time is taken to devise alternative solutions.
- Ideas are enhanced because a range of alternative solutions have been analysed.

- Can be time-consuming to gather information and carry out the analysis.
- Choosing from a range of solutions can be difficult to do in practice.
- Creativity and gut reactions to problems can be stifled.

(d) (i)
- Discounted prices will encourage people to buy more. **6**
- Discounted prices may sell more volume but not value.
- Loss leaders may encourage people to buy the goods and other things available in the shop.
- Some customers may only buy the loss leader on which there is no profit.
- Buy one get one free means the organisation makes less profit (reduces averall GP margin).
- Customer loyalty to the product may be established.

(ii)
- High expenses. **4**
- Too much cash tied up in stock.
- Customers not paying within agreed credit period.
- Drawings too high.
- High interest repayments on loans.

(25)

SOLUTIONS

Marks

36 *(a)* (i)
- Flat structure will allow for quicker communication and decision-making. **6**
- Can react quicker to changes in the external environment.
- There is less rivalry between departments.
- There are more opportunities for developing team-working.
- There will be some instability and inefficiency during changeover.
- Additional training may be required.
- The span of control will increase, leading to greater pressures and stress.
- A lack of supervision and leadership may lead to inefficiencies.

(ii)
- Used when the organisation is involved in a number of large projects. **3**
- It is useful for staff development.
- Can develop closer relationships with customers.
- It is easier to identify customer needs now and in the future.

(b) (i)
- Offering financial or non-financial rewards for achieving targets; and appraisal schemes. **4**
- Offering training schemes to allow for staff development.
- By having promotion routes for employees.
- The use of quality circles to involve them in decision-making.

(ii)
- Enter into negotiations to try and resolve the situation. **3**
- If no agreement can be reached, they may seek arbitration.
- Arbitration is where an independent arbitrator, such as ACAS, will listen to both sides and offer a solution.
- Arbitration may be binding, where both parties agree beforehand to abide by the arbitrator's decision.

(c)
- Piecework – where the employees are paid for each good unit that they produce. **6**
- Bonus – where employees are paid an additional payment when they achieve set targets for sales or production.
- Performance-related pay – where employees can get additional payments for doing their job well.
- Profit-sharing – where employees are given a share of the profits that the business makes.

(d)
- The organisation has an effective corporate culture. **3**
- The organisation offers good promotion prospects.
- The organisation offers a good financial package and other benefits.
- The organisation has a good training and staff development programme.

(25)

SOLUTIONS

Marks

37 *(a)*
- Legislation requires products to be advertised in an honest way. The Advertising Standards Authority monitors advertising, and if an advertisement is found offensive, the advertiser can be asked to withdraw or change the advertisement. **6**
- Both departments have to comply with the discrimination acts when recruiting, training, promoting staff etc.
- Health and safety legislation affects both functional areas in the supermarket – operations perhaps more so when food handling legislation has to be considered.
- Machinery, e.g. meat-cutting machines must be clean and safe for employees to use.

(b)
- The employer must provide a safe working environment which complies with the legislation. **4**
- It is the duty of every employee to act safely and look after their own safety and that of other employees. They must abide by the rules set out by their employer.

(c)
- The more stages in a channel of distribution, the more expensive it becomes. **7**
- Manufacturer loses control over marketing his own product.
- More personal service and advice for customer.
- Retailers provide consumer with information about the product.
- Retailers store, price and display goods.
- Retailers may offer consumers credit terms, after-sale guarantees and delivery.
- Manufacturer has guaranteed contract.
- Manufacturer sells more goods at a time.

(d) (i)
- Newspaper articles may contain bias or inaccurate information. **4**
- The story may be told in such a way that it sells a newspaper.
- Television interviews allow people to be heard 'live' so that what they have to say cannot be edited although they may try to cover the truth.

(ii)
- Relaunch product, with a lot of media coverage explaining that the problem has been solved. **4**
- Repackage the product.
- Have celebrities involved showing their use of the product.
- Offer guarantees, e.g. money back if not satisfied.

(25)

Marks

38 *(a)* (i)
- Extension strategies – these may involve improving the product, changing the packaging, changing the price, changing the advertising, producing product line extensions. **5**
- Competitive pricing – ensuring that the price charged for the product is the same or lower than the competition.
- Promotional pricing – the price of the product is reduced for a short period of time, to generate higher sales and regenerate interest in the product.

(ii)
- May be the only company with a product in that market segment. **3**
- Ability to make large profits by avoiding competition.
- May be identified as the market leader for such products.
- Build expertise in one type of product/consumer market.

(b)
- To become the market leader in a particular area **3**
- To stay ahead of the competition
- To develop new and more efficient techniques

(c) (i)
- Allows targets to be set **4**
- Identifies possible problem areas
- Can be monitored weekly/monthly/annually
- Allows decisions to be made in advance

(ii)
- Bank overdraft – allows short-term cash fix at relatively low cost. **3**
- Trade credit – allows the organisation time to pay for items purchased from suppliers.
- Retained profits – the organisation may be able to access profits retained from previous years.

(iii)
- To compare performance across different years within the organisation **3**
- To compare performance with other similar organisations
- To identify trends over a period of time
- To inform future decisions

(d)
- Centralised structure – control and decision-making lies with senior management based at head office. This is similar to a hierarchical structure. Staff who are not involved in the decision-making process have little authority. **4**
- Decentralised structure – control and decision-making are delegated to departments, which removes the responsibility from senior management. Subordinates assume responsibility, and the process of decision-making is quicker compared to a centralised structure.

(25)

SOLUTIONS

SOLUTIONS

				Marks
39	*(a)*	(i)	• Works councils are formed from the workforce and are involved in the decision-making process in the organisation. • They have the right to access information from their employers. • Their involvement will improve relations between employers and employees. • Employees will be more motivated due to their involvement. • Their rights are protected under EU legislation.	**4**
		(ii)	• The organisation may have an effective corporate culture. • Here the workers feel part of the organisation and are keen to work towards their objectives. • Good communications policies will ensure that the workforce knows what the employer is trying to achieve. • They will have a better understanding of decisions. • The organisation has a good training and staff development programme. • Offering good promotion prospects, a good financial package and other benefits.	**4**
	(b)	(i)	• The organisation will have to assess the impact of their operations on the environment. • They will become involved in the local community – sponsoring events, setting up partnerships with schools, etc. • They will become involved with initiatives within their industry, e.g. reducing additives in the food industry. • They will communicate their intentions to the public through the PR department. • They will improve the working conditions for their employees. • Working with pressure groups within their industry.	**5**
		(ii)	• The quality of information available • The ability of the decision maker to take risks • The experience and qualities of the decision maker • The ability of the decision maker to use decision-making techniques • Personal interest of the decision maker	**4**
	(c)	(i)	• They can provide a high degree of personal service. • Customer loyalty can be built up. • Responsive to the customers needs. • Higher staff costs. • Can be more difficult to control. • Duplication of some functional areas will be necessary.	**4**
		(ii)	• Functional grouping – the business forms into departments around the main functional areas such as marketing, human resources. • Product/service grouping – here the business organises around the different products that it produces, setting up divisions for each product grouping. • Place/territory – the organisation organises itself around the different areas that it operates in, to better meet local cultures or tastes.	**4**
				(25)

				Marks
40	*(a)*	(i)	• A job description is a description of the job vacancy, stating the title, location, tasks, duties and responsibilities of the post. • A person specification details the type of person that would be suitable to fill the vacant post. It describes the qualifications, experience, personal qualities and interests that the ideal candidate would possess.	**4**
		(ii)	Induction training for new staff is important as it covers background information about the organisation, procedures, health and safety, introduction to colleagues and an introduction to the main points of the job.	**3**
		(iii)	Options for the organisation include: • Negotiation – the employer and employees jointly discuss matters arising of concern to both sides, in an attempt to meet a mutually acceptable position. • Arbitration – where negotiation has been exhausted, arbitration involves the use of an independent third party who considers both sides and gives an impartial solution, to which both parties agree to abide.	**5**
	(b)	(i)	• Hierarchical structure – this is the traditional organisational structure containing many levels of management. Decisions are made by senior management and are communicated down the chain of command. This means that communication may be slow, resulting in resistance to change. • Flat structure – this has few levels of management, meaning that information can be passed quickly and effectively between levels. There is more independence between departments.	**4**
		(ii)	De-layering involves removing layers of middle management (and flattening the structure of the organisation) to reduce costs and improve efficiency.	**4**
	(c)	(i)	A takeover is when one organisation takes complete control of another organisation.	**2**
		(ii)	• Grant – a source of finance from local or central government. This is usually a one-off payment. • Retained profits – profits kept in the business from previous years can be used to fund future expansion. • Bank loan – money can be borrowed from a bank and repaid over a fixed term plus interest. • Share issue – a limited company (private or public) may issue shares to raise funds for expansion.	**3**
				(25)

SOLUTIONS

Marks

41 *(a)*
- Use the media to cover good work being carried out. **3**
- Employ a public relations officer who may make a statement, apologising to the media.
- Dismiss any employees involved and make it known to the press.
- Employ a famous patron who has a good personal image.

(b) (i)
- Reliable in that a record is kept and it can be referred to again. **5**
- It may not be accurate.
- It may contain author bias.
- It may be out of date.
- It may have been gathered for another purpose and not suitable for the user's needs.

(ii) Oral **6**

- Information can be given in presentations (e.g. charity dinner speeches, television interview).
- Good for passing information quickly to charity workers, e.g. by telephone.

Pictorial

- Images of animals in distress can be shown to the public and the message understood much more quickly than by a written statement.
- Can be helpful when language barriers make communication difficult, e.g. working with people in countries where charity support is needed and English is not the main language.

Graphical

- Can be used to present information to show trends, e.g. 'the number of people receiving help from a charity has increased'.
- Allows comparisons to be made.

Numerical

- Allows financial information to be shared with donors.
- Statistics concerning the amount of people requiring help can be communicated.

Quantitative

- Information which is measured and can help an organisation to analyse it and make forecasts, e.g. '35 per cent of the people in South Africa…'

Qualitative

- Expresses opinions in words and is descriptive, e.g. 'I think that the work being done…'

(c) Trading, profit and loss account **6**

- Shows the profit or loss over a period of time
- Shows income and expenses
- Gross profit is the difference between the cost of goods bought to sell and their selling price
- Net profit is gross profit with expenses deducted

(Charities/clubs may not produce profit and loss accounts but calculate a surplus of income over expenditure in a statement called an income and expenditure account.)

(d) A partnership is most likely to be a business which sets the objective of profitability, growth or increasing market share. Partnerships could have the objectives of any business – to be the best, to launch a new product, to enter a new market. **5**

A charity aims to help a needy cause by raising money or obtaining donations. Their objective is to provide a service.

(25)

Marks

42 *(a)* Go slow **6**

- Employees do their jobs but very slowly.
- Slows down production rate.
- Sales levels may fall.

Overtime ban

- Employees refuse to work overtime hours.
- Some work will not be completed on time.
- May affect late delivery penalties.

Work to rule

- Employees only do what they have to.
- May reduce productivity.

(b)

- To ensure that they have sufficient staff with appropriate skills **4**
- To manage employee relations
- To maintain the commitment of the workforce
- To manage employment legislation within the workplace
- To manage remuneration and appraisal schemes

(c) Health and safety **9**

- Employers have to raise the standards of the health and safety of employees.
- Machinery has to be properly maintained.
- All hazardous substances are dealt with properly.
- Risk assessments have to be carried out for all employee tasks.

Employment

- Men and women doing similar work have to be paid the same.
- They must ensure there is no direct or indirect discrimination in terms of sex, race, disability and age.
- Must ensure that they pay at least minimum wage.
- Must meet the requirements of the working time regulations.

Use of ICT

- Must meet the requirements of the Data Protection Act.
- Must provide regular breaks for those working on PCs.
- Have to provide suitable lighting, ventilation etc.
- Must provide suitable equipment (e.g. adjustable seats).

(d)

- Downsize – reducing the scale of operations to meet actual demand and focus on core activities. **6**
- Reduces staff costs.
- Allows the business to be more efficient.
- May mean the closure of productive units.
- Empowers remaining staff.
- May lead to lower morale and conflict.
- Redundancy payments will have to be made.

(25)

SOLUTIONS

Marks

43 *(a)* (i)
- To stay ahead of and compete with the competition **4**
- To attract the best staff
- To be more efficient
- To reduce costs and save money
- To increase productivity

(ii) Computer Misuse Act 1990 – governs the use of computers, the internet and email. **6**

Data Protection Act 1998 – affects the storage of personal data held by organisations.

(b) (i) A mission statement is a clear statement of the organisation's reason for existing. **2**

(ii) A mission statement is important because it addresses the organisation's basic need for definition and direction. It should also clearly communicate the organisation's purpose to its customers. **3**

(c) (i)
- To review individual performance over a period of time. **3**
- Good performance can be rewarded.
- Training needs can be identified.

(ii)
- Performance targets are known. **3**
- Rewards for good performance/meeting targets are known and achievable.
- Increases staff motivation

(iii)
- Needs analysis will be carried out. **4**
- Timescale for improvement/further review can be carried out.
- Training can be organised.
- Further poor review/failure to meet targets set and agreed may result in disciplinary action/dismissal.

(25)

Marks

44 *(a)* (i)
- On-the-job training is training carried out at the employee's normal place of work. **4**
- Off-the-job training is training carried out at a different location from the normal place of work, e.g. training centre.

(ii) Costs **5**
- Financial
- Staff may need time away from normal work duties
- Better trained staff may leave for better work with another employer

Benefits
- Increased staff motivation
- Staff become more competent
- Staff become more productive

(iii)
- Allows feedback to employees on their performance **4**
- Allows targets to be set
- Raises awareness of performance targets set by employers and to be met by employees
- Allows review of past performance
- Acts as a motivator to staff

(b)
- Strategic decisions are long-term decisions usually made by senior managers, e.g. to improve efficiency. **6**
- Tactical decisions are medium-term decisions which are mainly about how to achieve the strategic objectives set by the organisation, e.g. if the strategic objective is to improve efficiency, then the tactical decision may be to cut staff numbers.
- Operational decisions are short-term (often day-to-day) decisions made by managers responsible for the day-to-day running of the organisation, e.g. organising staff cover, placing an order for consumables.

(c) (i)
- To ensure entry is made to the market **3**
- To raise awareness among consumers
- To demonstrate how/why this product differs from its competitors
- To gain sales

(ii)
- Newspaper/magazine adverts **3**
- Television advertising
- Outdoor media
- Sales promotions
- Direct mailing

(25)

Marks

45 *(a)*
- Penetration pricing can be used when entering the market. **7**
- Destroyer pricing can be used to remove a competitor.
- Promotional pricing can be used to encourage customers to buy.
- Loss leaders can be used to encourage customers into the store.
- Increased advertising may increase custom.
- Development of product endorsement, produce placement.
- samples, BOGOF etc.

(b)
- Increased competency of staff. **6**
- Increased flexibility.
- Increased staff motivation.
- Increased production.
- Easier to introduce change.
- Improves image of organisation.
- Financial costs involved.
- Loss of work time.

(c)
- Widens labour pool. **4**
- May need to be flexible regarding working hours.
- Demand for crèches, sports facilities, health products etc increases.
- Need to be competitive (consider product, price, promotion).

(d) (i)
- Inexpensive. **5**
- Questions designed to find out what you want to know.
- Relatively easy to collate.
- Can cover a wide geographical range.
- Tick boxes make it easy to complete.

(ii)
- The correct segment of the market is targeted. **3**
- Saves wasting money asking the wrong market segment.
- Interviewer can substitute another person when someone is not in.

(25)

SOLUTIONS